THE
WINNING EDGE

THE WINNING EDGE

DON SHULA
WITH LOU SAHADI

E. P. DUTTON & CO., INC. | NEW YORK | 1973

Acknowledgments:

Special thanks are due Joseph Robbie, the managing general
partner of the Miami Dolphins, for the efforts contributed by
two members of his front office staff—Director of Public
Relations Mike Rathet, who coordinated the entire project,
and one of his P.R. aides, Diane Hayes.

Published simultaneously in Canada by
Clarke, Irwin & Company Limited, Toronto and Vancouver
ISBN: 0-525-23500-0
Library of Congress Catalog Card Number: 73-9318

For my wife, Dorothy, and our children, David, Donna, Sharon, Anne and Michael, who have shared the frustrations and are now having the opportunity to join in enjoying the ultimate—a world championship.

1

Sleep did not come easily. I had been tossing and turning for over an hour, trying desperately to fall asleep and put things out of my mind. I had never experienced a night like that before. It was all so strange, lying in a motel room in Long Beach, California, the night before the 1973 Super Bowl, tossing, turning, praying everything would work out well for us the next day. It was the most important game of my career. I felt more pressure than at any other time in my life.

The game itself, against the Washington Redskins, was one thing. I had coached in two previous Super Bowls, in 1969 and in 1972, and had lost both. That bothered me. I didn't want to lose a third time. I felt confident, but there was always the fear that something would go wrong. I was proud of the way the Dolphins had played all season long. We had won sixteen games in a row, something that no other team in the history of professional football had done. Yet, it

1

wouldn't mean anything if we lost the next day. The whole season, everything we worked for, would be wasted. As a coach you learn to live with game pressure. But, something else, something not directly related to the playing of the game itself, really disturbed me. It stuck in my throat and it was too bitter to swallow. Just a few days before, Carroll Rosenbloom, the owner of the Los Angeles Rams, had made a slur on my character. My ability as a coach is one thing. An attack on my character as a person is another. Through it all I had to remain virtually silent. It wasn't a pleasant position to be in and most certainly not before the biggest game of my career.

I had coached for Rosenbloom a few years back when he was the owner of the Baltimore Colts. We had a pleasant relationship then. But that was three years before. During the intervening years, Rosenbloom kept criticizing me whenever he had the opportunity. The remarks hurt not only me but also my family. I had never attempted to retaliate before, but now it was getting to me, making me feel bitter inside.

During the middle of Super Bowl week I became terribly upset by a newspaper column in the Baltimore *Evening Sun* written by the sports editor, Bill Tanton. The article was picked up by the Miami *Herald* and reached me in Los Angeles on Thursday.

The column quoted Rosenbloom as reiterating what he had said before the season, "That it would be just his luck to have these two teams wind up in the Super Bowl." Tanton said that he could understand why Rosenbloom was less than ecstatic about seeing Shula win the Super Bowl but what about Washington? Then Rosenbloom, in his own style, went on to say that "these are two coaches who broke all the rules in football." He said that all Allen did was cheat on some rules involving waivers, which left me stunned. The inference was that I had done something even worse.

The article was particularly upsetting because my entire family was in Los Angeles with me. Rosenbloom was accusing me of breaking all the rules in football and then making me look even worse by saying that the only thing that Allen had done was cheat on players. It meant that I had done much more than that. My oldest son, David, who is thirteen, heard about the article and had read it before I had an opportunity to talk to him about it. He was asking me questions and searching for answers.

"Dad, I always thought that you were honest and as fair as you possibly could be," he began.

"That's right, son."

"Yet, in the newspaper Rosenbloom says that everyone knows that Shula and Allen have broken all the rules in football. What does it all mean?"

"I've always tried to do everything according to the rules, David. If I've broken any rules, I don't know about it."

He seemed reassured.

"I'm sure of that, Dad," he said smiling.

"I'll find out the answers, you can be sure of that."

It was really disturbing to have my son inquire as to what rules I had broken as a coach in professional football. I always want to be able to give my son an honest answer as to what type of person I am and more important what type of father I am.

I immediately made my feelings known to Commissioner Pete Rozelle. I was not about to remain quiet on another attempt of character assassination by Rosenbloom. It wasn't the first time he had done this to me. The commissioner said he hadn't read the article, so I proceeded to read it to him over the phone. I didn't want to wait for a private meeting. This concerned me and my family and I wanted answers right away.

I told him that my children, particularly David, the youngest, Michael, who is seven, and even the three girls, Donna, Sharon, and Anne, were all very curious to know what rules their daddy had broken. I stood accused, but without charges. My wife, Dorothy, who has been through this before because of earlier attacks by Rosenbloom, was asking me, "When is it all going to stop?" I firmly told Rozelle that I was at a loss trying to explain to my children about the inference that I had broken rules. They were entitled to know what it was all about because I would like to think that I am bringing up my kids the right way. Now they had read that their father was dishonest and they wanted to know why he was being accused. Rozelle said he would look into the matter and get back to me. By that Saturday night, I still hadn't heard from him.

All these thoughts raced unchecked through my mind as I tried to sleep the night before the Super Bowl. I tried to analyze the events that had transpired over the past few days. Would they help or hurt the

Dolphins' chances tomorrow? The more I thought about it, the more relieved I was. Rosenbloom's remarks, coming when they did, might even give us an edge. In the three years since I left Baltimore, the Dolphin players had become sick and tired of hearing all the accusations Rosenbloom threw at me. In those years I have tried to treat my football team as honestly and as fairly as I possibly could, asking only that they judge me by my actions.

I was certain that my relationship with the players has been a good one. Although Rosenbloom's remarks disturbed and upset me, I sensed that they would have a positive effect on the players. I felt that the players were waiting to show the world that the Miami Dolphins were ready not only to play for the world championship but also to win it and help put to rest the stigma that I was a coach who couldn't win the big game.

As I tried to sleep, I thought back to the two weeks before the Super Bowl when we began our serious preparations for the Redskins. I had regrouped my squad on a Wednesday at Biscayne College, which is located in North Miami, just three days after we defeated the Pittsburgh Steelers for the championship of the American Football Conference. We were in a unique situation. Although we had won all fourteen regular season games and two playoff battles for a 16–0 record, a loss to the Redskins in the Super Bowl would wipe out a season-long string of successes, all the good things that we had accomplished. It was a season that had been filled with a great deal of personal accomplishment. We broke the NFL team rushing record by gaining 2,960 yards, and we had two runners, Larry Csonka and Mercury Morris, gain 1,000 yards or more for the first time in history. I collected my one hundredth victory in the ninth game of the season against the New England Patriots, the first time any coach had every posted one hundred victories or more in his first ten years of coaching.

But we all realized that these honors would only be really meaningful if they came within the framework of a world championship season. All of our energies, all of our dedication, was directed toward that goal. We hadn't succeeded the previous year against the Dallas Cowboys, but we were determined this time, even more so in the wake of that loss.

The bitterness of the 24–3 loss to Dallas had a lasting effect, probably more so because we never challenged in the game. We had opportunities early but never took advantage of them. Trailing only 10–3 at half time, we felt we could still come out and win. But instead of taking control, we let the Cowboys dominate and just completely run the ball down our throats.

The most disappointing aspect of the Dallas game was that we never showed people we belonged in the Super Bowl that day. Instead of walking away from it as proud world champions, we came away as disappointed losers. I didn't want that to happen again. We had too much at stake to go that route once more. The squad was reflective that Wednesday. It has always been able to learn from adversity. We pointed to the bitterness that we experienced in the loss to Dallas in

Super Bowl VI as the final stepping stone to the world championship in Super Bowl VII. The game would be especially meaningful to me. If we lost, I would have been the first coach in history to be 0–3 in Super Bowl play. I would have hated to be introduced at banquets around the country as the only coach that had lost three Super Bowl games—but then I probably wouldn't have been invited to any.

My first decision was a big one—I had to decide who the starting quarterback would be against the Redskins —Bob Griese, who was just coming back from a broken ankle, or Earl Morrall, who did an excellent job taking over for Griese. It was a vital decision that could affect the final outcome of the game, yet I had to make it. Not on the day of the game, but now. There wasn't any time left to wait. I wanted to begin practice that afternoon with the problem settled. Then there wouldn't be any doubt cast over the workouts, which would make for better practice sessions. After the morning meeting was over, I called Griese into my office.

"How do you feel?" I asked.

"I feel fine, coach."

"Any physical hurts from the Pittsburgh game?"

"No, I'm real good."

"How's the ankle?"

"The best it's felt since I hurt it."

"Good enough to start in the Super Bowl?"

"I'm ready to play if that's your decision."

"Well, Bob, I am thinking very seriously about starting you."

Griese's eyes lit up. It was easy to see how keyed up

Bob was. I walked out behind him and looked for Morrall. I wanted to talk to him privately and to inform him about my decision. How do you tell a guy who led you to eleven straight victories that he was going to be benched? Being the man that he is, Morrall understood my decision. But I knew that down deep he was disappointed. His performance enabled us to get into the Super Bowl. But it was a fact that in the last few games we were having trouble getting across the goal line and that caused me to make the decision to start Bob Griese.

I explained to Earl that the big reason I made the decision was that I felt our team would be stronger with a healthy Griese starting. I wanted Earl ready to come in just in case something happened to Griese or because he wasn't getting the job done on the field. I much preferred having Morrall in reserve rather than Griese because, due to Bob's inactivity, I wouldn't really know what to expect if he got into the game.

I left myself open for criticism. A lot of people second-guessed me because they felt that similar decisions had backfired on other coaches who had recently switched quarterbacks. The week before, Dallas, with Roger Staubach at quarterback, had looked very bad against the Redskins. Coach Tom Landry decided to start Staubach after considerable inactivity and to bench Craig Morton, the quarterback who had done a good job for him. Staubach showed signs of rustiness and never did get the Cowboys off the ground.

The same thing had happened with the San Francisco 49ers a couple of weeks earlier. Coach Dick

Nolan had to decide between starting veteran John Brodie or Steve Spurrier. Brodie was coming off an injury and Spurrier had done an excellent job in his absence. Nolan went with Brodie and as it turned out, the 49ers lost to Dallas.

Judging by the results, I might have been inclined to stay with Morrall instead of starting a rusty and inactive Griese. But I believe that you have to make every decision based on the merits as they affect your team, and that's exactly why I made Griese the starting quarterback. Despite the second-guessing, I didn't have any misgivings from the time I made the decision right up to the game itself. I was confident Griese could get the job done.

And so our squad went to work with Griese as our No. 1 quarterback and Morrall as the backup. We had spirited workouts in Miami for the remainder of the week. On Sunday, we left for Los Angeles and our final week of preparations for the Redskins. It is a league rule that you have to take your team to the site of the Super Bowl a week early. I don't necessarily agree with it. But the league insists that the time is needed for press conferences and to enable the players to prepare in the atmosphere in which they are going to be playing.

I feel that arriving at the site that early is a little too much. I particularly think that the press conferences early in the week can be done away with. They don't serve any important purpose. There should be a concentrated period of two days in the middle of the week when the players and the coaches are available for in-

terviews. After that they should be left alone to prepare themselves completely and in private for an
opportunity to play and win the Super Bowl. The
chance doesn't come along that often. Anything that
distracts you from this opportunity is harmful, particularly when you work so hard to get there.

I was very encouraged by the attitude of the team.
We had apparently been loose the week before we
played the Cowboys in Super Bowl VI, but this was
different, more natural, no forced humor. It was probably because of the fact that we had been there before
and had gone through the routine of the press conferences and other demands made on the players. Actually, we have a relaxed group of individuals. We try
to be honest and act the way we normally do. This is
the image that I like to project to our players and they
seem to respond well to it.

The honest, relaxed mood of the team was very evident at our first meeting in Long Beach. We were
scheduled for a press conference at 1:00 P.M. I called
an impromptu squad meeting to get the players together and explain some of the time schedules we
would be responsible for the rest of the week. As I
looked around the room, I noticed two players, center
Jim Langer and guard Bob Kuechenberg, were missing. We waited for them to come. But, we didn't send
anyone to look for them because it wasn't a scheduled
meeting and they probably couldn't be found.

I thought this was a good opportunity to have a little
fun. A few minutes later, Langer and Kuechenberg
walked in the door and all the players turned around. I

looked at my watch, gave them a dirty look, and pointed at the two chairs that I had turned facing one of the corners in the room. I instructed them to sit in the chairs facing the corner with their backs to the rest of the team, like they used to do in school to punish a young child when I was a kid. This, naturally, brought quite a bit of reaction from the squad. It really loosened them up. They jawed on and on about Langer and Kuechenberg being late, teasing that they were late because their massages took a little bit longer than they normally do in the massage parlors that are prevalent in the Los Angeles area. As it turned out, Langer and Keuchenberg were actually in a health studio working out with weights.

As the week progressed, I understood from the newspapers that Allen was going exactly the opposite way. He talked all week long about the distractions and the time-consuming press conferences, about how much they were interfering with his schedule. My attitude hinged on the fact that I realized that these were necessary things that you were asked to go through. That's the way it was done in the past. So, I played it down as much as possible with my team. I asked them to cooperate during the designated times and pointed out that they were free to do what they wanted to do with their leisure time.

I tried to keep my press conferences light and, in particular, to make it an enjoyable experience. As long as I was facing an army of reporters, I wanted to be as informative as I possibly could. I didn't want to drag it out or make it appear that I was uncomfortable or didn't want to be there in the first place. I wanted to appear loose in contrast to the tightness that Allen displayed. I felt that it would help our squad in its preparations.

I also realize that Allen has been highly successful because he works so hard and does everything that he can possibly do to get his team ready to win. I thought that he was using some of the distractions as a method of emphasizing to his team that they had to concentrate and work much harder in order to overcome them. I think that is why he hit the distractions so hard as opposed to my approach, which was to soft-peddle them.

I've always had a good relationship with George. We've probably talked on the telephone more than any other two coaches—and with the least amount of results, I might add. I've only managed to negotiate one small trade with him. I've talked to him about a lot of big ones and yet never completed one. At league meetings or coaches meetings, any time that we've had the opportunity, we've always sat down and talked football and organization. I enjoy talking with him because he's a guy who has been successful. I'm always eager to pick up things that he's doing and I'm not. I'm sure he feels the same way about things that we talk about. But although we have spent all this time talking together, I don't really know George well.

Despite my respect for George, I don't condone some of the things he's done. I feel that the league should have caught him a lot quicker than they did when he traded draft choices he didn't have. Now, the league is much stricter.

Our practice sessions went well. Our preparation was pretty much the same as it has been throughout my coaching career . . . with one exception: this game meant much more to me than any other game I have coached. And I could sense that it meant more to our team than any other game that the Miami Dolphins had ever played.

The game plan we devised for the Redskins was not a complicated one. Offensively, the Redskins do not throw a lot of formations at you. Nor do they use a lot of fancy shifts or men in motion. They're a very basic football team relying on execution. Their whole theory offensively is not to make any errors, to control the football, to keep it away from the other team and then for their defense to completely overpower you. This philosophy worked very well for Allen in the two games prior to the Super Bowl. It probably was the main reason Washington was favored to beat us.

Washington played brilliantly against Green Bay in the first playoff game. They kept the Packers from scoring a touchdown and completely smothered their great running attack. The Redskins employed a five-man defensive line that seemed at times to upset Green Bay and force them to do things they weren't used to doing.

But the Redskins played an even better game against Dallas for the National Football Conference championship. They dominated the defending-world-champion Cowboys to such an extent that the game was over midway in the third quarter. It was sad to see world champions bow out the way they did. I hope my team is never in that position. If we do go down, I'd like to think that we'd go down fighting, scratching, and swinging, doing everything that we possibly can to win. The Dallas Cowboys did not go down that way. They surrendered to the Redskins in a manner that would have been very embarrassing had I been the person responsible for their performance that particular day.

We felt that the Redskins's plan would be to try to control the ball by establishing their running attack. During the season they ran with the ball much more than they threw it. Larry Brown carried the ball three times more than their other runner, Charlie Harraway. We were determined to stop Brown. We felt if we could, we could beat the Redskins. During our practice sessions we worked hard on preparing for Brown, the way he would start out running wide to either the right or left and then cut back. Duane Thomas of the Cowboys had been very successful with this maneuver against us in Super Bowl VI.

I had the defensive linemen concentrate on staying in their proper pursuit lanes, waiting for Brown to cut back while looking for the blocking from the offside. We worked long and hard to master this without getting cut down by a block. I emphasized one more thing. I told the linemen that if they did get knocked down by a block to get right up and not overpursue but to stay in their lanes and recognize that sooner or later Brown was going to cut back.

The secret in controlling the Redskins' quarterback Billy Kilmer was, first, to take away the running game, thus reducing the effectiveness of his play-action passes. Then, after doing this, to exert pressure on him when he attempted to throw from the pocket. Kilmer is not a good pocket quarterback. But he's a quarterback who understands the value of the run and mixes in the play-action passes. Occasionlly on first down, he'd just step back and fire the bomb to Charley Taylor, Roy Jefferson, or even tight end Jerry Smith. Kilmer likes to catch an opponent off balance this way.

In order to curtail their offense, we conditioned our defense to take away the short passes from Kilmer. We wanted to force him to throw the ball up and over the top of our linebackers where our deep backs had the opportunity to react. We concentrated on the passes that Kilmer likes to throw—the sharp, quick passes to the inside, the slant-in variety to either Jefferson or Taylor.

Kilmer is a quarterback who leads pretty much with his dedication and his willingness to gamble. He doesn't have the greatest amount of physical ability as far as running or throwing is concerned. That's why it was vital for us to take away his quick, short pass inside, to force him to set back deeper in the pocket and throw over our linebackers' heads into areas where our deep men were responsible. Let's face it, Kilmer doesn't have the strongest arm in the world. He is not accustomed to throwing the way we wanted him to, up and over. In this way, we reasoned that he would hang the ball in the air, giving our defensive backs and line-backers time to react. It would put us into situations where we could intercept and create turnovers, which would be necessary to keep the Redskins from control-ling the ball.

Offensively, our game plan was to take advantage of some of the things we knew about Allen and his method of preparing for a game. Allen is the most me-thodical coach in professional football today. He works harder and spends more time on tendencies and statis-tics than anyone I know. He breaks them down and then presents offensive tendencies to his defense. He wants them to recognize formations and know what an opponent's No. 1 tendency is, No. 2, No. 3, and so on. He starts out a game trying to stop your best receiver, your best running back, and tries to force you to do things that you are not accustomed to doing.

We figured that Allen would try to concentrate on containing Mercury Morris, who is a tremendous out-side running threat, while keeping an eye for Larry Csonka to run up the middle. As for our passing attack, we knew he would try to devise a way to stop our No. 1 receiver, Paul Warfield. We also knew that he had those charts on frequencies—how many times we ran with the football as opposed to how many times we threw the ball on first down. In the last three years we've definitely been a running team as opposed to a passing team, particularly on first down. Statistically, we employ the run on a 3 to 1 ratio on first-down plays. We felt that there was room here to take advantage of the situation since the Redskins would be expecting us to go along with what we had been doing all season long. So, I designed some play-action passes to use on first down and also to throw deep, hoping to catch them by surprise. I wanted to establish our running game and at the same time make our passing game work effectively.

There wasn't anything more I could do. All the preparations were done. The game plan was set. I didn't have any second thoughts about naming Griese to start the game ahead of Morrall. I knew the squad was ready. One more game, the biggest one I ever prepared for, and it would be all over. I wanted to win this game more than any other game of my life.

All I wanted now was sleep. That was the hardest part. I tried to dismiss everything from my mind. It wasn't easy. If my week hadn't been disrupted by the remarks that Rosenbloom made about my character, then I could have relaxed. But I was annoyed and aggravated. I finally managed to unwind. The last thing I remembered before dropping off to sleep was what Rosenbloom had said. He thought that I had matured some as a coach but that he'd seen me freeze up in the big ones and that until he saw it he wouldn't believe I could win the big one. I fell asleep determined we would win.

It was all up to the squad. I had no complaints about the weather or the squad, which looked loose the next day in warming up before the game in the Coliseum. It was a warm day and we are used to that kind of weather. When the players finished their warm-ups they returned to the locker rooms at the far end of the huge stadium. I called them together and asked the players to take a few seconds by themselves to think about how much the game meant to them, to bring the Lord into our lives. After I allowed each player these few precious seconds, I led them in the "Our Father." They all joined in. When we finished reciting the prayer, I allowed them a few moments to finish praying on their own.

Then I began my pre-game talk. I informed them that we had won the coin toss and would receive, emphasizing how important the special teams are. Then I gave them instructions on our first series of plays. The thinking was to start with probably our most basic play, a bread-and-butter one. It was a run with our line firing straight out at the Washington line and Csonka going one way, with Jim Kiick taking a jab step and then getting the ball and following the blocking of the line. Because of the type of play I wanted to begin with, I decided to start Kiick ahead of Morris. Kiick is better geared for this type of power play. I felt this particular play was the best way to release some of the nervousness the players usually have in the initial series of the game. I also wanted to test the Washington team, to make them realize that we would come after them with everything we had. If we win on that first play, driving them back off the ball and making four yards or more, then it's a successful play. If we don't, it's evident that they are keyed up for the game a little more than we are. As far as I was concerned, it was very important that we get started the right way on the very first play of the game.

Our second play was selected to take advantage of their eagerness. On this play, our line was to set as if it were a pass play. However, instead of Griese fading to pass, he would slip the ball to Csonka who then hits the hole as the blocking takes place. The name of the play is "25 lag give-it." Normally, the play calls for a draw to the halfback with the halfback getting the ball after a fake to the fullback. But this time I wanted the fullback to carry the ball to take advantage of the over-eagerness of the Washington defense.

After establishing what I wanted on the first two plays, I then discussed our first possession situation. Any time we are faced with a third down and three yards or more to gain, we consider it a possession situation. We have to gain the yardage to maintain possession of the ball. In such a situation, I prefer the pass more often than the run. In a long possession situation, I told Griese to use a slot formation. In this setup, we take out the tight end and insert another wide receiver, Otto Stowe, on one side and put Paul Warfield in the slot and Howard Twilley outside on the other side. If the situation were a short possession, third down and three or four, I pointed out to Griese that a quick screen to the fullback with two linemen out in front and a halfback leading would be a good play.

I also had a short-yardage play set up for the first series. Again it was a basic play. But this time I wanted Morris to carry the ball out wide with straight blocking by our line, tight end Marv Fleming hooking their linebacker, Csonka leading the play, and Morris ready to cut off the block. The players sat there nodding quietly. They understood what I wanted done in given situations.

After I finished explaining the first series of plays, I could still see the anxiety and the tension in the room. I emphasized that we were going after victory No. 17; the climax to a great year—the greatest year the National Football League has ever known; and the third of the three goals we wanted to achieve when the season began. I restated the goals briefly. The first, of course, was to qualify for the playoffs. The second was to win the playoffs and get into the Super Bowl right here where we were today. And, finally, the third goal was to win the World's Championship, which would mean that the Miami Dolphins would be recognized as the greatest team ever—17 and 0!

I then pointed out that the lessons we learned in the past would help us through the tough periods of the game. We could reach back for confidence and call on the experience we had gained by having been through it once before. The one experience that no one knows unless he has been there is the feeling we had been subjected to after the Super Bowl the previous year when we played a disappointing game against Dallas. That loss stayed with us all year long along with the realization that when it was all over there weren't two outstanding teams anymore, just one . . . the Super Bowl champions. The other team joins the pack, along with the other twenty-four. They are all lumped, all twenty-five of them, all inseparable, chasing the No. 1 team, the world champions. I reiterated that we had reached the Super Bowl by being solid in every department and by being people who care for each other and who would win for us. I stressed victory No. 17, a Super Bowl win over Washington, would give our team what it deserved—a world championship and a new page in history.

There was nothing more to say. It was time to assemble on the field for the battle. As I walked up the long tunnel, I couldn't help but think that this was it. The whole season has come down to one game. The season-long success, the records, the 16–0 mark all hung in the balance. If we lost, the whole campaign would be a bust. Nobody would remember the sixteen victories. They would all point to the one loss. I wanted so badly to win just one more time. It would be beautiful, an unbeaten campaign capped by the world championship.

We got it. And I still can't explain the feeling. I just felt relieved of a lot of pressure, like a steam pipe bellowing smoke into the sky. I was happy for the squad, for Joe Robbie, the owner of the Dolphins, who also had to endure countless criticisms over the years, for myself and my family. Now, no one can deny what my team and I had accomplished.

It is just amazing how fate focused everything on that one game. It reached a point, despite all the success of the past, where I needed that one victory to be exonerated. I felt that pressure right up to the kickoff. But once the action began, I never thought about it again. I was too immersed in the game itself. Fortunately, everything went the way we had planned. We wanted to surprise Washington and we succeeded. Our first touchdown came in a situation where the Redskins didn't expect a long pass. Griese threw a perfect pass to Twilley who put a great move on cornerman Pat Fischer, got open in the corner, and scored a touchdown.

On a couple of other occasions, we called play-action passes on first down and caught them flatfooted. However, we were unable to capitalize on all the opportunities that we created because of two costly penalties. Griese completed one pass that was a big gain only to have the play nullified because we had linemen downfield. And there was a touchdown pass to Warfield that was called back because of an offside. We had worked hard on the play in practice and finally reached a point in the game where it was ideal to use. Warfield worked his way behind the secondary and was wide open when he caught Griese's pass. However, Marlin Briscoe, our other wide receiver, was offside. In his eagerness to get downfield to occupy Fischer and keep him from dropping off on the ball, he jumped before the ball was snapped. The penalty cost us a touchdown. Naturally I was disappointed. It was an easy touchdown. I was upset with Briscoe when he came to the sidelines.

While these were costly mistakes, I still had the feeling that we were doing so many positive things that the game was turning in our direction. We were able to hang onto the football, establish our running game, and at the same time make our passing game work with great effectiveness. But, in addition to the two penalties, there were a couple of things that happened that kept us from breaking the game open. One was an interception on second down and five on the Washington five-yard line. The play was a calculated risk one and possibly not a good percentage play. We were ahead 14–0 at the time and had to get at least a field goal out of the situation. But I felt it was an excellent time to get a touchdown and Griese felt the same way. We went with the play-action pass but, unfortunately, Griese underthrew Marv Fleming and Brig Owens leaped in front of him and intercepted the ball. The play kept the Redskins in the game; they were down only 14–0 when they could have been behind either 21–0 if the play worked or 17–0 if we went for a field goal.

The other play that hurt was the most talked about one of the entire game. I know it gave me some anxious moments near the end. We were still leading 14–0 with only two minutes left when Garo Yepremian, an excellent field goal kicker, brought the entire crowd up on its feet. It was a play that developed from a chain of events. I thought long and hard before making the decision to go for a field goal. I realized that the only way the Redskins could get back into the game was to block the field goal attempt and score a cheap touchdown. But I looked at it positively: Yepremian gets the ball up in a hurry and gets good height early on his kicks; normally our center snap is good; our line is a fine field goal protecting one and the chance of blocking the kick was actually very low because of the way we execute on field goal protection.

So, I decided to go for it because I felt that if we did

get our lead to 17–0, the game would be out of reach. However, the snap was a little bit to the inside and low, and Morrall had trouble handling it. When he finally positioned the ball, Yepremian kicked it low and our line had a breakdown in protection. The Redskins got penetration and blocked the kick.

I couldn't believe it. I immediately thought about the worst thing that could happen, and that was the Redskins picking up the ball and getting the cheap touchdown. As I was thinking about it, I saw that the ball was bouncing in our direction. I remember looking up toward heaven to thank somebody, because certainly that was a stroke of luck. As the ball bounced toward Yepremian, I found myself sighing in relief knowing that Garo would grab the ball, fall down on it, and protect it. Before I knew it, however, Yepremian picked the ball up on the run and tried to adjust to throw a pass. I couldn't believe my eyes! What is he doing? I just stood there in bewilderment. As he raised the ball, it slipped off his hands. While still in the air, Mike Bass caught it and ran for a cheap touchdown. The worst possible thing that could have happened had happened.

Yepremian was totally embarrassed as he trotted off the field. I felt terrible for him because he had contributed so much to the success of the Dolphins over a period of three years. But he certainly shouldn't have tried to make the play that he made. It all stems from a soccer player being put into a football situation and not ever having faced the incident. In our practice sessions occasionally we'll throw in some unusual plays that could happen in a game. But there was no way you could ever practice for a situation like that. Besides, Garo had been told that if anything ever did happen that he couldn't control, he should fall on the football and protect it and we'd take our chances after that. But he thought he was doing the right thing at the time—and may have visualized either throwing a touchdown pass or at least grounding the ball so it would revert to the line of scrimmage. In his mind he thought he was right. I guarantee it will never happen again.

Right after that the Redskins had a tough decision to make. The score was now 14–7 and they had two alternatives. One was to go for the onside kick. The other was to kick the ball deep, hold, get field position, and try to score the touchdown that would tie the game and force it into sudden-death overtime. It was too upsetting to think about. I certainly wanted to prevent such an ending. I had another quick decision to make. I sent our short field goal team on the field and alerted them for the onside kick.

Allen, however, decided to kick the ball deep. Maybe he figured that we were prepared for the onside kick. Possibly he reasoned that if he had tried the onside and it had bounced in our direction, then we would recover and could run the clock out without any problem at all. As it turned out, his strategy almost worked. They kicked deep and prevented any strong runback. On first down, we didn't gain much yardage. But on second down, Griese stepped back and calmly hit Warfield on a down-and-out pattern. It was a real gut throw. How many other quarterbacks would risk putting the ball in the air in that situation? But we noticed that they were blitzing and their cornermen were playing inside of our receivers. It was a matter of picking up the blitz and throwing the ball accurately. Griese had confidence that his blockers could pick up the charging defense and he also had confidence in his own ability to throw. The play picked up some valuable yardage and got us further out of the hole.

But we then found ourselves unable to move and had to punt. The Redskins came with a rush. But Larry Seiple, who is a pressure football player, calmly punted the ball out of danger. The kick carried into Washington territory. It was all up to the defense now. When Washington put the ball in play, they didn't have any time-outs remaining. The defense's job was to keep them inbounds and kill the clock. We employed a three-man line, our "53-defense," and they carried out their assignment. We were able to get good coverage on their receivers. At the same time, our three-man rush of Vern Den Herder, Manny Fernandez, and Bill Stanfill put considerable pressure on Kilmer. On fourth down, with everything riding on the final play, our coverage was tight. Kilmer hesitated and our rush swarmed all over him. The game was over!

That's when all emotion broke loose. Our team had been heavily criticized off and on throughout the year for not showing any emotion, for being very methodical and businesslike. And, after some significant victories during the season, we did seem to take our string of successes in stride. The thing that no one realized was that our whole season was directed toward what had happened on the field in the Super Bowl game on this particular day. That was our ultimate goal. But the emotion was there, on the sideline, running off the field, and in the locker room. We finally toned down a bit after some uninhibited jubilation mixed with some tears. We got back to business. The first thing we did was to take a few seconds on our own to say thank you and to think about some of the things that happened out there on the field. We took extra time this Sunday because of the tremendous things that happened to us, and each man in his own way thanked God for what this game meant to him.

For me it meant a great deal because of the tremendous amount of pressure that I had been subjected to going into the game. There is no minimizing the relief I experienced. No one could really feel what I went through. It was an emotional experience that I hope I never have to go through again.

The players were also relieved, undergoing the pressure of an unbeaten season. They, too, didn't want to belong to a team that had been to the Super Bowl twice and come away empty. They wanted the big ring because they had to settle for the little one the previous year. They executed brilliantly this time and because of that they actually made the Redskins look inept. It caused people to say that it was a dull game. And if those people were looking for a more evenly matched game, then certainly they had to be disappointed. Although the final score was 14–7, the score could have very easily been 21–0 at half time and we could have gone on from there.

I was proud of the squad. They did whatever it took

to win. They made the positive plays, gambled because they believed in their ability, attacked the Redskins instead of waiting for them to make mistakes. I was probably more proud of this than any other single thing in the game: the fact that our team went out and pressured the Redskins into errors and didn't wait for them to make them.

Overall, I thought our preparation was excellent. I felt the game meant more to us than it did to the Redskins. I also felt that our play under pressure was such that we deserved to win. When you go back and review the things that happened, it was clearly evident that we were the team that should have been the World Champions, a team that produced a 17–0 record—the perfect season.

2

My father was a Hungarian immigrant who came to Grand River, Ohio, with his parents when he was six years old. Grand River was a small fishing village of about 500 people located about two miles from Painesville, which was a town of about 15,000 to 18,000. Although my dad never mastered his adopted language and left school after the sixth grade, the people in the town thought enough of him to elect him to the town council.

Our name in Hungarian was Süle, but my father's first-grade teacher had trouble pronouncing it and changed the name to Shula. My dad was quiet but a tough disciplinarian. My mother made most of the decisions around the house, but when dad spoke, we listened. You knew damn well he meant what he said.

I was born in 1930 and was the youngest of three kids before my mom had triplets. I was fairly close to my older brother, but since he was six years older he

29

usually went his way while I would end up playing
with kids my own age. The Depression hit us hard.
Dad was making $15 a week as a foreman in a nursery.
After the birth of the triplets, who caused a lot of excitement as the first set of triplets to be born in that
area for a long time, dad realized that he would have
to get a job that brought in more money. Fortunately,
he secured one with a fish company. He would report
to work early in the morning, hop on a boat, help cast
big nets into Lake Erie, and begin to haul in the fish.
They would bring their catch to the fish house where
the fish would be filleted, frozen, or packed in boxes
covered with ice and shipped away. It was a long
day. My father would get up real early in the morning and wouldn't get home until late in the afternoon.
The only consolation was that dad was getting more
money now, about $32 a week. With six kids at home
it still wasn't very much. My grandparents' grocery
store certainly looked good to us.

Although my mother was also Hungarian, she was
born in America. Her parents had migrated from Hun-
gary and like my father she was a strong-willed in-
tensely moral person. My mother was raised a Catholic
and my father converted to Catholicism when he married her. A great many of the ideas and thoughts
that I have, as far as my relationship with God, stem
from those early years and the lessons I learned around
the house about being God-fearing and doing things
the right way. We never missed mass. From second
grade on I went to a Catholic grade school and even

today I try and attend daily mass. My mother was a proud woman. Even though money was scarce, I always remembered having clean clothes to wear. She made sure that if there were any rips or tears in our clothes that they were always sewn and that the buttons were always on.

What amazed me as a child was that nobody could go into the living room. It was strictly taboo. The only time it was used was when there was company. Otherwise, it was nothing more than a show place with everything in its proper place all neat and clean. I could never understand it. We did most of our living in the basement. It was fixed up and painted and we had a stove down there where my mother often cooked. Football has been so good to us that Dorothy and I have a rule that any time any of our kids want to play anywhere in the house they can—even if they want to throw a ball around. David learned to catch in the front room. But if I had tossed a ball in my folk's house, watch out.

We were a close-knit family. I always had to answer to both my father and my mother and they were demanding. I had rules and regulations I had to abide by. One I'll never forget: any time that the street lights came on, I had to come home no matter where I was. That was the signal. Lights on, I come home. One night the street lights never did come on because of an electrical failure and I didn't come home until very late. I was severely reprimanded by my parents. They asked me why I thought I could stay out that much after dark. I said that the rule was when the street lights go on I come home and the lights didn't go on. It didn't save me from a pretty good spanking.

The fortunate part about the area where we lived was that the grade school was right across the street. It had a good-size yard and we made ample use of the playground. There was always a gathering of kids and some kind of game going on as far back as I can remember. Even though I was much younger than the other kids, I was always allowed to play with them because I was a pretty good athlete no matter what the sport. I spent all my spare time in the playground. I didn't have any ambitions other than to play ball— football, basketball, baseball, whatever season of the year it was. The playground meant action and competition. Anything that interfered with sports upset me. Going home to eat was only a necessary evil. My parents didn't try to stop me from playing. Their only concern was that I was eating too fast.

Because of my early participation in athletics, I was a leader in grade school. However, going to junior high I soon discovered that there were many kids a lot bigger than I was. I wasn't the big star anymore. I was just another person competing for the team. At the end of the year I was one of twelve or thirteen chosen from the freshman team to compete against the varsity and finish the season with them to prepare for next year.

My football career almost ended then. I was playing defense during a practice session. The tight end caught a short pass and I came up and made the tackle. There was a sharp object on his uniform that was apparently being used to hold it together. As I made the tackle, this sharp object cut the side of my nose and ripped it open. It wouldn't stop bleeding. The coaches decided to send me to the hospital. When I got there they examined the gash and agreed that I didn't need any stitches. They bandaged it close together so there wouldn't be any scar. With that big bandage on my nose, I began to think of what my parents would say. My mother was waiting for me when I got home that evening.

"Donald, what happened to you?"

"Oh, it's nothing, Mom."

"What do you mean it's nothing? What happened to your nose?"

"I hurt it playing football."

"Let me see."

"Mom, it's really nothing. I'm okay."

"Don't tell me you're okay with a bandage that big. Your nose must be broken."

"No it isn't, Mom. I'm okay now, honest."

"Take that bandage off and let me see for myself. What will your father say?"

"All right I'll show you that there is nothing wrong other than a little cut."

As I began to remove the bandage, my mother was looking straight at me. When I got it off and she saw the gash, she slapped her face with both hands.

"Dear God. What kind of a game is this where you get bruised and battered like that? That's it. As far as I am concerned, there will be no more football."

"Ah, Mom, it isn't that bad."

"That's final. No more football. Now go wash for dinner."

I didn't put up much of a fuss. It was about the end of the varsity season anyway.

The following year I decided to go back out for football. When I brought a card home for my mother to sign to grant permission for me to play, she refused. My father also agreed that I shouldn't play football anymore. I ran out of the house with tears in my eyes and took a long walk. I decided that I wouldn't let anything stand in the way of playing football. I decided to sign the card myself without my parents' knowledge. This was the first time that I actually disobeyed them. But I loved the game too much to give it up.

Just before the start of the season, I came down with a case of summer flu that almost turned into pneumonia. I was in bed for a week. I had lost a lot of weight. But I felt I had to report for practice. It was a very hot day and in my weakened condition I wasn't able to compete at all. The second day was just as hot and I wasn't feeling any better. In fact, I felt even weaker than the day before. I wasn't doing very well and was discouraged. I told the coach that I didn't feel that I could compete and was turning in my uniform. I felt awfully lonely sitting up in the stands the first game of the season, watching players on the field that I had gone all through grade school with.

One day during gym class we started a touch football game. Our instructor was Don Martin, who was also the assistant football coach and the head basketball coach. After class he came up to me.

"How come you're not on the football team?"

"Well, I was out for a couple of days but I had to quit because I was too sick and couldn't compete."

"I don't remember seeing you at practice."

"The way I played nobody would remember."

"I don't know what happened then but starting tomorrow I think you better turn out for practice."

"Okay, coach, I will."

The next day I went out for football again. I made enough of an impression on the head coach, Clarence Mackey, to be added to the team. I felt great. I had been so unhappy when I had to give it up. But now that I was well again and could play, I felt good all over. I still didn't tell my parents. I just reported to practice every day without their knowledge. I began to do so well that the coach told me he was going to start me in the next game. Now I had to tell my folks. They couldn't believe that I had been playing football again. They realized they couldn't make me quit because I was so determined to play. I asked them if they would please come to the next game and watch me play. They agreed. This was the first time they had ever attended a football game. During the game, I returned a punt seventy-five yards for a touchdown. The fans were excited over the run and my folks became part of the excitement. From then on they became enthusiastic fans. They didn't miss any of the games and even started to travel with the team during our out-of-town games.

If it weren't for Don Martin, I might still be sitting in the stands. During high school he worked a lot with me on the football team. I played on his basketball teams. He also was the track coach and through Don I learned just how much dedication and sacrifice meant in order to be able to compete in this one-on-one sport. The personal sacrifice that's necessary in track taught me a great deal about competition.

Even when I was much younger I had always wanted to compete in athletics. There was an organized league in Painesville that consisted of fifth- and sixth-grade teams combined. My first coach was Joe Jenkins who was a former high school player who had a good way with kids and gave willingly of his time to help coach St. Mary's Catholic grade school team. It was eight-man football and I was one of the two backs. We had uniforms but you had to supply your own equipment. We had some fine teams in my early years and the competition in its way was as fierce as you could find.

I remember how much I wanted to win when I was in the sixth grade. We were playing for the championship. We didn't play too well, however, and got beat. People tried to console me after the game but, instead, I retreated to a position underneath the grandstand and wouldn't come out. I just cried my heart out feeling sorry for myself about what happened that day. I just couldn't hide my disappointment. Even then I had put so much emphasis on winning. There are many times when things don't go so well that I still feel like running and hiding.

My grandmother was the one who discovered my intense desire to win when I was a youngster. She was a gregarious woman who often would invite her Hungarian friends to come over and spend the evening and play a friendly game of cards. They used to play a game called five hundred. There were times when they couldn't get enough for a fourth. They would then send for me because I knew how to play. It was a game of partners. On many nights we would just begin playing and the cards wouldn't fall in place and we would get beat badly. I couldn't take it. They all knew that I had a hair-trigger temper and that I hated to lose. So, they would begin to laugh a little about it and get me going. I can remember taking the cards, after maybe only one or two games, and throwing them over the room stomping out and going outside to cry. I couldn't stand losing, and the teasing and ridicule that went along with it made it worse. I would like to think that I have matured a little since then and can handle a defeat, although I still hate to lose.

That even went for fighting in the playground. I was always pretty much able to hold my own in fights. I certainly won more than I lost. And there were plenty of scraps. There was one kid who was much bigger than I was who lived just one house away. We were great friends, but it seemed as if every day we would end up in some kind of battle. I got to thinking that I was pretty tough until one night I was challenged by this boy who was a pretty quiet guy. We squared off and the next thing I knew I was laying flat on my back seeing stars. I got back on my feet and got stretched out again. That's the first beating that I ever took. It really put me in my place a little and made me realize that I couldn't go out and lick the world.

I was always more interested in sports than in school. I never did bring books home. But in the classroom I worked hard and was able to keep pace. Yet, I never felt that I really gave as much as I should have to my studies in order to get the maximum out of them. Still, I always managed to do well enough to be in the top part of the class. I used to do all the odd jobs that I could after school. I would always bring the money home and give it to my mother. When I was twelve, I had a job that paid me a dollar a day. At the end of the week I'd give my mother the five dollars and she would give me fifty cents as my allowance. The rest she would put into a savings account so that some day, in case I needed it, she could help. She almost made me cry my senior year in high school. I was able to get a car because my mom had saved enough money. I played first string during my final two years in high school. In the last year, when our school tied for the league championship, I was named to the all-league team.

Yet, despite the fact that I also lettered in basketball, baseball, and track, there weren't any colleges knocking down my door to offer me a scholarship. The only way that I would have the opportunity to attend college was through an athletic scholarship. Scholarships were scarce at the time because all the veterans were returning from service and the college coaches were gearing their scholarships toward older and more experienced men. I finally received an offer from Emory and Henry College. My high school coach had gone there and told me that he could get me a full-tuition scholarship, but that was all. I would have to take care of my own living expenses. Then I received a partial track scholarship from Ohio State. With only these offers, I decided that it was best to stay out a year and work and get enough money so I could pay my way to a college of my choice the following year.

One day, early in the summer, I pulled into a gas station and saw Howard Baughman, a former coach of mine in high school. He had coached me as a freshman and left for a position at Cleveland Heights High School in Cleveland.

"Say, I've been following your career in high school and you did quite well."

"Thanks, coach, I'm glad you didn't forget me."

"What college are you going to?"

"I didn't get any worthwhile scholarship offers so I decided to go to work instead."

"That will be a mistake, Don. You should go to some college."

"But, where can I go?"

"Well, I know Herb Eisele, the coach at John Carroll University, quite well. Let me talk to him about the possibility of getting you in school there."

"That would be just great."

"Okay, I'll let you know in a couple of days."

Baughman did set up an interview the following week for me and a good friend of mine, Roy Kropac. The interview went well and Eisele offered us tuition scholarships. John Carroll was a pretty expensive school and Eisele's offer was a fair one: if we did well on the freshman team, we would get a full scholarship the remaining three years. John Carroll was within driving distance of Painesville and we could arrange a car pool with a couple of other kids attending the school so it wouldn't cost as much all around. After giving it a lot of thought, I decided it would be better to accept Eisele's offer than to stay out of school a year. Who knows what will happen in a year?

It was 1947 and there were a lot of good athletes returning from service. Still, I competed on the freshman team and did well enough. Carl Taseff, who later was to become one of my closest friends, had begun school the semester before and was eligible to play on the varsity, yet as far as class level was concerned, he was still counted as a freshman. We had an excellent squad. The quarterback, Rudy Schaffer, had a scholarship to Notre Dame. However, he didn't like it too well and decided to transfer to a smaller school. Eisele was very pleased with our progress in the scrimmages against the varsity. At the end of the season, he restated his promise that he would provide me with a full scholarship my sophomore year.

During my freshman year they had a three-day retreat on campus conducted by a Reverend Clark Cook who had spent a great amount of time in Chicago working with prisoners on death row. He was a very intense person. I was so taken with his account of his work that I was about ready to follow in his footsteps. What kept me from pursuing this feeling further was the fact that I wouldn't be able to continue my career in athletics. I felt I could be involved in athletics and still be religious, but if I decided to become a priest, I couldn't be an athlete. Besides, because of my inability to carry a tune, I would never be able to sing a high mass.

In my sophomore year I made the varsity. I lived on campus and became more involved in college life. I was a second-string halfback behind a senior named Jim Moran. I didn't get to play very much in our first game, but Moran got hurt and was sidelined for the next game. Eisele told me that I would start against Youngstown the following week. I was scared. Here I was given the starting assignment in the second game of my sophomore season. What if I failed? However, once the game started, I was all right. It was a hard-hitting game, the kind that I like. I played the entire game and carried the ball often. I gained 175 yards from scrimmage on twenty-five carries. I also scored both touchdowns in our 13–7 victory, one on a run and the other with a pass. It was a tremendous start, and from then on I was the starting halfback the rest of the season. We did well in the remaining weeks. Eisele was an exceptional coach. He only had two assistants but they were as fine a small college staff that you could find anywhere. Eisele completely adopted the Cleveland Browns' style of football, both offensively and defensively. He and his staff would watch the Browns's practices, see their games, study their style, and emulate it because it was so successful. They also taught fundamentals very well. The basis of my football training, which later enabled me to compete for a job in the pros, was started in my sophomore year.

During my junior year I suffered a number of injuries, the most damaging one being cracked ribs. They take an awful long time to heal and I was sidelined most of the season. I hated being out of action, but the injury was painful. Every time I took a deep breath the pain would shoot right through my body. I had to write off the year.

I was looking ahead with great expectations to my final year at John Carroll. So was the rest of the squad. We had a lot of veterans back for the final season. We worked hard in our off-season programs to try to get ready for spring practice and later the fall. I couldn't wait to play, to make up for all the lost time I experienced my junior year. However, we lost our opening game and then lost the next week. Before you can say win, we were 0–2. But then we started to get things turned around. We began to win consistently, and Taseff and I were having good years, gaining a lot of yards. I still continued to play both ways. Whenever Eisele felt I needed a breather, he would pull me out and try to rest me a little when we were on defense. Playing both ways gave me great opportunities to really learn the game.

The biggest highlight of my career at John Carroll was in my final year. It came against Syracuse University. We had a built-in incentive against Syracuse. When the game was scheduled, the Syracuse newspaper said in its headline: "Syracuse Schedules John Carroll." Right underneath that: "Who Is John Carroll?" Naturally Eisele clipped it out and placed it on our bulletin board. It was there all season long and we couldn't wait to play them. It turned out to be the biggest and best game John Carroll ever played. We beat them, 21–16 and convincingly so. We gained a lot of yardage on the ground and I accounted for 125. It was a very emotional and physical game. I got so exhausted because of the tremendous anxiety welled up in me and the ferocious play that I got hit so hard that I didn't know where I was. I had to be dragged off the field and I couldn't remember what quarter it was or the score of the game. But, they couldn't keep me out. I went back in after one play. What excitement erupted after the game was over. Little John Carroll had beaten mighty Syracuse. We finished our season 8–2.

Because Syracuse was so highly regarded, the entire Cleveland Browns's coaching staff scouted the game. I think that even Paul Brown was there himself. They obviously were scouting Syracuse for the approaching college draft. They were a big-time college team with a lot of material.

I wanted to play pro ball. I could only hope that some of the Brown coaches noticed me that day.

3

The first time I met Paul Brown I stood there shaking. Carl Taseff and I had been drafted by the Cleveland Browns and I couldn't have been any happier. We were anxiously waiting for the Browns to contact us after reading about it in the newspapers, but weeks passed and nothing happened. I couldn't take the suspense any longer so I called them myself. They told me that they were waiting until track season was over before contacting me. I felt greatly relieved to say the least.

I stood in Brown's office in the summer of 1951 completely in awe of the man. He was practically a legend and I had tremendous respect for him. I always watched the Browns play whenever I could. There were times when I had to cheat a little because I didn't have enough money to buy a ticket. I would sit in the end zone pretending to be a high school player so I could get in the stadium for twenty-five cents. Most of the time I had to scrounge up the money, but it was the best quarter I could ever spend. I had been a Browns fan all my life and now I was going to play for them. I was almost too excited to talk and just listened to everything that Brown was saying.

He offered us each a contract for $5,000, which we accepted in a hurry. I couldn't wait to sign. I kept worrying that at any minute Brown was going to pull the contract away. I was actually waiting for him to say that the Browns had changed their minds and decided not to bring us into camp. Nowadays players, no matter where they come from, a big college or a little one, have agents or lawyers negotiate for them. It's an altogether different game today than it was in those earlier years. I just appreciated the opportunity to play and had enough faith in management to feel that they would treat me fairly and honestly. And I certainly believe Paul Brown did that.

Taseff and I left Brown's office and burst into joy. We slapped each other on the back. I told Carl that I still couldn't believe it, we were pros.

"This calls for a celebration, Carl."

"What do you have in mind?"

"Let's just stop in the first bar that we see and have a drink together."

"Fine with me."

"It shouldn't be too difficult finding a bar in Cleveland. This is the big time."

"You better believe it."

"Do you think they'll recognize us as being new members of the Cleveland Browns?"

"You gotta be kidding, Don."

"Let's order something special."

"You're right. How about a couple of martinis?"

"You ever had one?"

"No, did you?"

"I never had one either. But let's celebrate in style."

We toasted each other. I took a big gulp and almost threw up. It's the last martini that I ever drank.

Taseff and I agreed that we would begin getting in shape before we reported to training camp. We wanted to be ready. The Browns were a solid veteran team and making the club wouldn't be easy. I'd drive to Cleveland to meet Carl and we'd both go over to work out with some of the Browns that lived in the area. Dante Lavelli and Cliff Lewis helped us and offered encouragement, and we all turned out to be pretty good friends. Being able to practice with some of the players really helped us. We learned quite a bit in those early workouts and got to know what to expect when training camp opened.

In those days the Browns trained at Bowling Green University. Naturally, the rookies were assigned to the top floor of the four-story dormitory. It goes without saying that the veteran players like Marion Motley, Otto Graham, Mac Speedie, Dante Lavelli, and others were quartered on the first floor. I learned fast that being a veteran meant something. I also learned that it would be tough making the squad. The rosters at that time only listed thirty-three players. Besides all the rookies on hand, there were a number of players in camp who had played with other teams before they disbanded. One of them was a fullback by the name of Chick Jagade, who later made the team. He was a powerful guy, real tough. When Brown pointed to a brick wall, Jagade would go charging into it and try to knock it down.

Carl and I spent all of our time together. We shared the same room. It was a great feeling just to have someone to talk to. I used to think that something was wrong with me because none of the veterans would ever talk to me. It's pretty much the same situation today. The veterans hold back any conversation until a rookie makes the team and proves himself. Then he is accepted. But fortunately I had Taseff. We were as close as could be. Some of the other rookies were pretty much on their own and it could get lonely at times. Nobody saw the veterans much after practice. They were the ones with the cars. They would take off and go in all different directions, and very rarely did they invite you to join them.

Two of the veterans, Lou Rymkus and Lou Groza, got to be quite friendly with us. Later we found out why. Rymkus would always invite Taseff and me out. We'd end up in a saloon where the bartender would always pass out cigars to the Brown players. Rymkus was a heavy cigar smoker. The owner would come over and gives us all cigars. Rymkus would then get us back in a corner and take our cigars away. And that would be the last time we saw him that evening. He'd thank us for the cigars and take off in his car. Taseff and I were left on our own.

But, we really didn't have a lot of time for outside

activities. We were concentrating on making the team. The Browns were primarily interested in me as a defensive back and were a bit impressed that I knew the types of defenses they used since I played both ways in college. This got my foot in the door initially, and I was determined to make the most of it. Taseff was moved over to offense and was doing quite well. He appeared to have a shot at making the squad.

I remember the thrill I got lining up one day, when Otto Graham asked me to catch a few balls. It was during the early weeks of camp. I was a guy from a small college who had the opportunity to catch passes thrown by a star of Graham's magnitude. It's much different now. The rookies report to camp much more versed in what's going on than we were. We just walked in starry-eyed and hoped somehow to do something that would catch the coach's attention. We had nothing else to worry about but studying our playbook and getting ready for the meeting and the practice sessions, so that we would have the opportunity to compete. And that's all I wanted to do.

The Browns appeared pleased with me. I made a good impression on Blanton Collier who was the defensive backfield coach. Boy, was I ever thankful that my college coach, Herb Eisele, had adopted the Browns's system. It provided me with such a solid background. I was making good progress until the Browns became aware that the National Guard unit that Taseff and I belonged to would be activated before the season started. Since I faced the prospects of not being on the squad, the Browns started to work with another defensive back, Ace Loomis. As the days rolled by, Loomis was getting more and more playing time. I was getting discouraged because whatever you did well was noticed by the coaches and I wasn't getting much of an opportunity to do anything.

One day during a scrimmage I was sent in to play middle safety. The ball was snapped and our linebackers were wiped out. Motley had the ball and broke through the line. Now, Motley to me was one of the greatest running backs of all time, up there with Jimmy Brown, the best I've ever seen. He weighed about 245 and had great speed. Motley was an awesome sight when he broke through the hole in what the Browns referred to as a trap draw. Now he was coming at me in full stride, looking to run right over me. I had to stop him. It was just the two of us in the open field. I came up to meet him, force against force. I lowered my head and put everything I had into the tackle. I wrapped my arms tightly around his legs and Motley went down. What a feeling of satisfaction I had. All of a sudden I heard Paul Brown's voice.

"Nice tackle, Taseff!"

I couldn't let that pass, not after the tackle I made. I looked back and yelled.

"It's not Taseff who made the tackle, it was Shula."

Paul Brown broke into a laugh.

As we approached our last pre-season game, I went to the National Guard armory to get a clarification of my status. I knew the Browns were concerned and I didn't want to lose the opportunity to play because of it. I asked the officer in charge of the unit for a ruling.

I told him my pro career was at stake. Realizing this, he guaranteed that if the unit was activated during the season, Taseff and I wouldn't have to report until it ended. I asked him to contact Brown and notify him, which he did. It made life that much easier. Now I had a better opportunity to win a job. The Browns wouldn't have to worry about me not playing out the season. I later found out that one of the veterans, Tony Adamlee, who was captain of the team, recommended to Brown that I be given a final opportunity to make the team. Brown respected the opinions of his veteran players and Adamlee felt that I was a better player than Loomis. Brown then told me that he would give me a final shot. He would start me against the Los Angeles Rams in the final pre-season game. And if I did well, it would certainly enhance my chances of making the team.

Everything was riding on that one game for me. It seems that every now and then in life you get into a situation where just one event can actually determine the direction that your life will take. I was too young to realize it then, but that was the situation I was facing. In the game I was playing against one of the great receivers of all time, Tom Fears. The Rams had a couple of excellent quarterbacks, Bob Waterfield and Norm Van Brocklin. I was certainly going to be tested. Fears caught his first pass on me. I came up and made the tackle and rolled over with him. He felt I was twisting his leg and he reached down and kicked me in the mouth and uttered some profanities. But I kept my cool. I knew I couldn't afford to start a fight and get

thrown out of the game. I would lose any chance then
of making the team. And believe me, it took all I had
to hold back and not swing at Fears. So, I remained
calm and played a pretty good game. I intercepted two
passes and made a big runback with one of them. I also
made some strong tackles on runners in the open field.
Still, I didn't know where I stood when the game
ended.

The system that Paul Brown employed with his players was different than with other coaches. After the
game, he told the players to report to his office in
Cleveland the following Tuesday. There he would
hand out envelopes to the five or six players competing
for jobs, notifying them of his decision. On the way
downtown I kept thinking to myself, "What if I don't
make the roster." Maybe I was wrong to turn down the
one job offer I got when I graduated from college. I
was offered a coaching job at Canton Lincoln High
School, which would pay $3,500 to $4,000. At the time
I thought it was a good opportunity to get started in
what would be my life's work, but that job was certainly filled by now. I had almost taken it back in June.
I knew that making the Browns's squad would be a
long shot. But I also wanted to try and play professional football. It was a decision that only I could
make. I didn't want to live the rest of my life second-
guessing myself wondering whether or not I was ever
good enough to play in the pros. I knew that the
coaching job would be gone but I felt that there would
be others. Right then I formed a philosophy in life that
has remained with me. I always want to do the best

that I can with the opportunities that God has given me. The only way that you can do that is to give yourself the chance to go as high as you possibly can. If you don't have the confidence in yourself and you don't have the desire to compete and move ahead, then you start to get stagnant. This is when you begin to second-guess yourself wondering whether you had done the right thing. Everything that I have done has always been predicated on doing the best that I can with the ability that God has given me, trying to reach as far as I possibly can. And if I fall a little bit short, then I'm still further ahead than if I hadn't reached at all.

My fate was all in the envelope that Paul Brown was going to give me. I was fairly confident of my abilities as a player but facts were facts. I was still a guy from little John Carroll University competing against guys from the Big Ten and the Southwest Conference, some of whom were All-Americas. Now I was ready to accept whatever the decision was because I felt I had done the right thing in trying to make the Browns's team. Brown gave a little talk and then handed out the envelopes. I nervously opened mine and once again anxiety was rushing through my body. I wanted so very much to play professional football. It was there for me to read. "Congratulations. You have made the Cleveland Browns football team. Report to the stadium on Wednesday morning for a meeting and practice at 9:30." I was the happiest guy on the face of the earth.

I began the season playing on the speciality teams and as a reserve defensive back. In the third game of the year, Tommy James, the regular defensive back, pulled a muscle in practice. He would definitely miss the game that week and maybe more than just one. I took his place—a rookie—suddenly a starting defensive back on the defending-world-champion Browns. It seemed that Paul Brown was intent on getting me ready for my first game. He directed all the pass routes that were thrown against me. In practice I had to cover our receivers in one-on-one situations. Each time that I failed to cover receivers like Mac Speedie or Horace Gilliam properly I would look back at Brown. He would be shaking his head and Collier would be doing the same thing. They must of had their doubts about me getting the job done. But when Sunday came, I discovered that I had a lot of help in the game. Our pass rush was fierce and the other defensive backs helped out. I passed my first test and that took a lot of pressure off me.

I was having a pretty good season. Even though I didn't play in the first two games or the last one, I ended up with six interceptions in nine games. The interception that I didn't get caused me the greatest disappointment. We were playing the Chicago Bears and early in the game they were on a drive deep in our territory. I intercepted a pass on the four-yard line and ran it back ninety-six yards for a touchdown. Then my heart almost dropped. I looked back up field and the referee was signaling a penalty. He called a roughing-the-passer infraction and called the play back. I was furious. I slammed the ball on the ground and walked back the entire length of the field, from one end zone to the other. I wanted to show my disgust. If the touchdown had been allowed, it would have been the longest interception in Cleveland history.

Another disappointment occurred as we were preparing to play the final game of the season against the Philadelphia Eagles. Brown called me aside one day at practice and said that I had been doing a fine job, but Tommy James was healthy now and he was going to start him and put me in a reserve role. Now, nine games later, games that we had won, I was back on the bench. Although I didn't agree with Brown's decision, I kept my mouth shut. But it hurt. Oh, how it hurt. I felt as if my world had collapsed.

Even though we beat the Eagles in the final game of the season for our tenth straight victory, the entire team suffered a disappointment in the championship game against the Rams. I didn't play until the final minutes, although based on my season's performance, I felt I deserved the chance to start. But I learned to accept Brown's decision. He was the coach.

But I still found some solace when the season was over. I was the only rookie to make the Browns that year. Taseff made it later, being activated from the taxi squad after the fifth game. So I was the only one who survived the cut. I was probably one of the youngest rookies around. I was only twenty years old when the season started. Now Taseff and I had to fulfill our military obligations. Our unit was activated and sent to Camp Polk, Louisiana. It was regular army life, but our thoughts were on football. We were wondering how long this would go on before our unit was deactivated.

We were then sent to Fort Bragg, North Carolina, to physical training school. This was very helpful to us because it taught Taseff and I a little bit about leadership. They trained us to be instructors and when the course was completed, we returned to Camp Polk. The physical training part wasn't too popular with the troops. They'd come in from the field after a hard day's maneuvers to find the physical instructors waiting. We weren't too popular with the troops to say the least.

The best part was when Taseff and I made the camp's baseball team. We were then placed in special services. It was a gas. We worked in an office in the morning and then had baseball practice in the afternoon. It was almost like being at training camp again. Vic Janowicz, who was an All-American football player at Ohio State, was on the team. In July, he got permission to leave camp and play with the College All-Stars against the Los Angeles Rams. However, we couldn't get permission to see the game. The major in charge of the baseball team sympathized with us. During a road trip, he put another member of the team in charge. We then jumped in his car and took off for Chicago to see Janowicz play. When we showed up, he was the most surprised guy in the world. All of us were A.W.O.L. We watched the game and left right after it and returned to the baseball team.

When the baseball season was over, we were asked to play on the division football team. However, we refused. But we offered to help coach. The reason we didn't want to play was that there was an excellent chance that we would be out of the army before the pro season began. That being the case, we didn't want to jeopardize our chances and possibly get hurt. As luck would have it, the Korean War ended and our entire unit was going to be deactivated. We wanted to return to Cleveland as quickly as possible. Our company commander helped by getting our release. I got discharged on a Friday and immediately called Paul Brown.

"I could be back in Cleveland for Sunday's game."

"You better get here quicker than that."

"What's wrong?"

"Tommy James just pulled a muscle in practice today."

"You plan on playing me?"

"Of course I do. What kind of shape are you in?"

"I'm in great shape. I've been working out and playing ball."

"Do you remember the defenses from last season?"

"How could I forget them?"

"Then get the first plane you can and see if you can be here tonight."

"I'll try. I don't know what the plane schedules are."

"Well, hurry and find out. I would like you to work out tomorrow. It will at least give you one practice day before Sunday's game."

Luckily I was able to get to Cleveland that night. On Saturday, I worked out with the squad. The coaches worked hard with me. They showed me a few things that they were doing a little differently than last year. It didn't take the Philadelphia Eagles long to test me. They were fully aware that I had just joined the team. Early in the game I had to make a tackle on Al Pollard. He kicked me in the mouth as I brought him down. He knocked my front tooth out, loosened another one, and severely cut my lip. It had to be sewn up completely. That finished me for the day. We had a good team dentist. He capped one tooth and replaced the other. He got me ready to play the following week with one of the new plastic bar face masks that had just come out. It enabled me to play the rest of the season without missing any games. Again we got into the playoffs and for the second straight year we came away disappointed. This time the Detroit Lions beat us for the championship.

After the season I returned to school. I was working on my master's degree in Physical Education at Western Reserve University. I was able to complete the work on my master's in two semesters. After one of my classes I stopped at the coffee shop. I bought a newspaper and ordered a cup of coffee. I turned to the sports page and did a double take. I slammed my coffee cup down, half spilling the contents. There was my picture along with several other players. I had been traded to the Baltimore Colts in a multiplayer deal! That's the first time I knew about it, reading it in the newspaper. I had mixed emotions about the trade. I was a local boy who had gone to a local college and played for a local pro team. Now, all of a sudden, I was being sent to Baltimore to play with a young football team in a city that was going to be completely strange to me. The only consolation I had was that my buddy Taseff was also part of the trade. It was really unique the way our friendship was able to continue.

I contacted the Colts and spoke with Don Kellett, the general manager. He was quite impressive on the phone. Of course, there wasn't anything I could do except to make the most of it. I couldn't worry about Cleveland anymore. That was my old team. I was now a member of the Baltimore Colts. Just like that. They had a new owner in Carroll Rosenbloom. That was the first that I had heard of him, though it most certainly wouldn't be the last. They also had a new coach, Keith Molesworth. So I signed my first contract with the Colts for $6,500. That was $1,000 more than I got with the Browns. In my second year with Cleveland, Brown had given me a $500 raise, to $5,500. So, to begin with, I was making more money.

When I got to training camp in 1953 I quickly discovered that I was doing more than competing for a job in the defensive secondary. The coach, Russ Murphy, wanted to do everything the way it was done in Cleveland. Only, he wasn't familiar with the Browns's system. He asked me to help. I was actually helping him with the planning and making corrections on the field. I started in the secondary. We did well in the pre-season and continued to do so in the early part of the regular season. We were known as the "Radar Corps" because we really zeroed in on the opposing team's passes and came up with a lot of interceptions and big plays. Then we played the Eagles who had a group of fine receivers, Bobby Walston, Pete Retzlaff and Pete Pihos. The Radar Corps cracked. They took us apart and beat us pretty badly. From then on until the end of the season we had trouble winning.

I returned home to Painesville after the season. I

didn't plan to do too much. Most of my nights were spent in a bowling alley. It was the gathering spot in town. We'd meet there and decide what to do for the rest of the evening. There was a bar there if we wanted to stay and have a couple of beers. And if there was nothing else to do, we usually ended up bowling a few games. One night three girls came in and bowled on the alley next to the one my friends and I were using. Like anything else, we started passing conversation back and forth. We introduced one another and one of the girls was Dorothy Bartish. This was the first time I had met her. I had heard her name ever since grade school, through high school and even college. But I had never met her even though she lived in the same town. Actually, I was four years ahead of her in school. During those years I learned that Dorothy's mother had died when she was born and she was raised by her Irish grandmother. Her father worked in the railroad yards and like mine didn't make a lot of money, but he always managed to set some aside so that he could send his daughter to college. I remember hearing how much John Bartish had sacrificed for his daughter and yet this was our first meeting.

We talked a little about college and then invited them downstairs for a drink. On the way out, I asked Dorothy for a date. She accepted and we decided to go out Saturday night. Early that evening I rang Dorothy's doorbell. Her grandmother, Mrs. Hammond, invited me in, but I felt that she was a bit cold toward me. I tried to start a conversation but I didn't get very far. Thankfully, Dorothy came into the room and told her grandmother good-by and we left for the evening.

When we got into the car, I asked Dorothy about her grandmother and why she appeared so cool. Dorothy laughed. First of all, she explained, her grandmother was as Irish as can be. Her maiden name was Fitzgerald. She had married an Englishman by the name of George Hammond. But she still had strong Irish ways. She disapproved of her daughter dating John Bartish, who was a Hungarian. Still, the couple wasn't discouraged. They decided if they didn't get her approval for marriage, they would elope. So they did. Dorothy's grandmother didn't accept Bartish until later. When her daughter died in childbirth, the split between the two widened. The grandmother raised Dorothy and naturally exerted a great amount of influence over her. She didn't approve of another Hungarian coming around and now dating Dorothy.

After that was settled, I sort of shook my head. I could understand her grandmother's feelings. But this was another time.

"What would you like to do?"

"What do you suggest?"

"How about a movie?"

"No. I'd rather not spend time in a movie."

"What would you suggest then?"

"Let's do something more exciting."

"Like what?"

"I like music and dancing."

"That's fine with me."

I didn't want to tell her then but it was entirely opposite of what I liked to do. If anything, I was a little shy and didn't have a great deal of confidence in my dancing ability. So, we stopped at a place that had dancing and ordered a few drinks. We had some great conversation and when the music began, Dorothy got me out on the dance floor and really helped me with my dancing. But the thing that I really liked out of all this was that she really opened up my personality. I was very happy with Dorothy on that first date. I needed someone like Dorothy to encourage me, to help me try new things.

We dated quite a bit that first year. Our relationship was growing stronger. Even though we both saw other people, we looked forward to the times we were together. However, Dorothy and I agreed that we shouldn't get serious about each other. She was going into teaching and I had to return to Baltimore to play football. And when I did, the Colts had a new coach. Rosenbloom had fired Molesworth, but kept him in the organization as the personnel director. He originally wanted to get Blanton Collier as his head coach, but Collier wasn't available and Weeb Ewbank got the job instead. Ewbank, of course, put in the entire Cleveland system. He had been exposed to it under Paul Brown and had also been Brown's personnel director. Ewbank is a very meticulous person who put in a great deal of time in planning and actually was the coach that the Colts needed at the time.

He did a good job, although our first game of the 1954 season was a disaster. The Rams, with Van Brocklin at quarterback, scored on the first play of the game and this was partly my fault. Ewbank had entrusted me with the responsibility of calling defensive signals. I had to come into the defensive huddle from my right cornerback spot and hustle back into position. After the first play I came in and called the defense and didn't see any outside receiver. I saw a receiver lined up tight on the weak side. I thought that I was on the weak side. But the thing that I didn't know was that the Rams did not huddle. They only huddled ten players and the eleventh one just stood on the sidelines near the other Rams players. He blended in with them real good. So good in fact that I didn't even see him. When the ball was snapped, Van Brocklin dropped back to pass. He threw a ball that must have traveled sixty yards in the air. I said to myself, Where can that dummy be throwing the ball? And I was amazed when I then saw a Rams player run under it, catch it, and run for a touchdown. I looked around embarrassed. Then I realized that this player didn't have to come into the huddle. He was allowed to line up as a player would for a sleeper play and this was actually the Rams's game plan. Throughout the entire game they only huddled ten players. The outside receiver would run out for a pass, or come over and throw a block on a running play. He would then leave the field and another player would step in from the outside and line up. I had to let a linebacker, Bill Pellington, call the signals in order to stay outside and be prepared to cover the player that wasn't huddling. Later, the league adopted a rule prohibiting this maneuver because they felt that every player should be required to take part in the huddle. It was a crushing defeat for

Ewbank. The team looked good in pre-season and had high hopes. But we bounced back and won some games and it was obvious that the Colts had the nucleus of a pretty good team. We improved in 1955, and in 1956 we really started to move. Johnny Unitas joined the team and so did Lennie Moore. The Colts's future looked good.

My future wasn't as good. I was really just an average player who knew what I was supposed to do out on the field. I enjoyed the contact and the challenge of learning my assignments but understood that I really didn't have that good a year in 1956. Most of the time I played with a badly sprained ankle that required injections before each game and this hampered my performance. I could see that the coaches weren't that high on my performance. Ewbank was turning more and more to younger players. During the 1957 training camp, I was beaten out of a regular job by Milt Davis, who was an excellent defensive back. Ewbank even decided to keep an untested veteran player ahead of me. He also rated a back by the name of Henry Moore over me. Near the end of training camp, there wasn't any room for me on the roster. I was cut. It was too late to get a coaching job. The only thing I could do at this stage was to try and hook on with another team. I was in excellent shape. All of a sudden I had the cold realization that I was no longer a part of the Baltimore Colt organization and this was a tremendous disappointment. I felt in the early years that I had contributed quite a bit to them. Now I was released just before the 1957 season with nowhere to go.

I sat up in the stands and watched the Colts open the season against the Detroit Lions. The Colts won and I went down to the dressing room to congratulate the players. I received the biggest surprise of my life when I walked in. The players presented me with the game ball. It meant a great deal to me. Even though I wasn't a teammate anymore, I was walking away with their respect. It meant more than anything else. It certainly helped lighten the anguish that weighed on me of being released and leaving a great bunch of guys who later were to become world champions.

During the week, I was picked up by the Washington Redskins. I joined them in time for the second game of the season. We were just an average team. Joe Kuharich was the coach and he was offensive-minded. We moved the ball pretty good but our defense didn't hold up. I didn't play too well against my old team, the Colts. Raymond Berry had an exceptional day against me, catching nine or ten passes. He set a record of thirteen receptions in the game.

I still maintained my closeness with the Colt players during the season I was with Washington. Whenever I had some off days, I would always go to Baltimore and spend my time with some of the players. I wanted to continue to hold onto these friendships because a lot of them were lasting ones. Our whole life then was football. We didn't want to do anything else. We weren't interested in outside business activities. The only thing that we were interested in was having training camp open and then competing to play. Very few of the players had any type of outside job at all. When the season was over, they would either go back to their home towns or stay in Baltimore and try to land some sort of job. There wasn't much television then and the game wasn't nearly as popular as it is today. The players didn't have a lot of opportunities that they have now, commercial endorsements, business tie-ins, the tremendous openings that are there for the professional athlete today. Two of the years that I had played in Baltimore I was a used-car salesman in Painesville during the off-season. When the Colts left the field for the day we all went to the favorite watering hole and had a few beers and discussed the things that happened that day. We would then go back to camp, have dinner, and go to the meeting together. After the meetings we would go out again, have a couple of more beers, and get something to eat until it was time for curfew. After curfew we'd get together in someone's room and tell stories about football. Everything was football, football, football.

Now when practices are over, the players scatter in all different directions. Now that I'm a coach, I feel that as long as these outside activities are not interfering with our performance, then I'll permit them. If they do, then I discourage them and tell the players to give their total concentration to our football program. If their outside activities are impeding this, then they must be stopped. A lot of players have radio shows, television shows, writing columns for periodicals, any number of things. The game has gotten so popular that the players are taking the place of movie stars. I want them to fully realize their business potential, but only as far as it doesn't interfere with the contribution to our football team. That's the thing that's most important.

Everything is so much better now than it was then. We try to do everything in a first-class manner: practice fields, training quarters, equipment, team meeting rooms, plane travel, hotels and such. Paul Brown was the one who started this practice. He believed that if a team was treated first class, they would perform that way. He paid the highest salaries because he felt that if he had a winning football team, they should be paid the most. As far as he was concerned Otto Graham was the best player in football and should be paid accordingly. Otto's salary was $25,000 or $30,000, which is just a drop in the bucket to what some of today's stars are getting.

Players coming into professional football today are more aware of what they are getting into. They know that they are going to utilize their years in the game as a springboard to future success in other fields or in football if they prefer to stay in the game. They are much more businesslike in their approach to football. We were more gung ho; we had more camaraderie. We enjoyed each other's company a lot more. The players today are all business on the field and certainly work as hard as we did, but they are more aware of the tremendous opportunities that they have at their fingertips.

So, I'll say hurrah for them and be a little envious

that we didn't have the same opportunities as players. But when you get right down to it, there's only one thing that is important. That's what the player does for you on Sunday—it better be there.

4

It was a strange feeling. I suddenly felt cold all over. I looked up on the big board that broke the squad down position by position and my name was below that of a rookie. At first I couldn't believe my eyes. I looked again, only this time harder. A rookie who hadn't played any professional football was rated over me. Had I reached the end of the road as a player? I certainly wasn't that old. I had played two years with the Browns, four with Baltimore, and one with Washington. That's only seven years. I was only twenty-seven years old. That's not old by pro standards. I couldn't be finished. Maybe I would be traded to another team if Washington didn't want me. Or maybe I could stay with the Redskins, fight for the job and beat the rookie out. Then I would have to do it again the next year with another challenger. If they rated a rookie ahead of me now, then I had a tough struggle ahead of me. I had to face the realization that maybe I didn't have it anymore as a player. Luckily I found out early, before training camp opened and it would be too late. I learned about my situation on a casual visit to the Redskins's office. I was driving through Washington and decided to drop by the office and say hello to the coaches. They invited me into their meeting room and that's when I saw the big personnel board for the 1958 season.

In my own mind I had figured to play just one more year. I had discussed the situation with Dorothy after the 1957 season. She, too, was in the process of making a decision. She wasn't too happy with teaching at the same school again. She had been accepted for a teaching position in Hawaii and had decided to go. On our last date we talked about the future and there wasn't anything definitely said regarding our relationship. We had agreed to write each other so we wouldn't lose contact. After all, playing another year in Washington would take me away from Painesville.

But all that would change now. I made up my mind when I left the Redskins's offices that I wasn't going to play anymore. When I got back home to Painesville, I made a couple of phone calls. I let it be known that I was interested in coaching because I had decided to retire as a player. Loving athletics the way I did coaching seemed to be a natural next step. Then I drove from Painesville to Philadelphia where the National Collegiate Coaching Convention was being held. I felt that if I talked to some of the people at the meetings and around the lobby, letting them know that I was looking for a coaching job, then my chances for getting a position would be better.

At the convention, I bumped into Frank Lauterburger who was an assistant coach at Army at the time. I knew Frank from his days as an assistant coach with the Colts when I was a player. I told him what I was looking for. He was surprised that I had decided to retire but said he would be glad to help me. Within a week I received a phone call from Frank. He told me that Dick Voris, a former assistant at Army, had just taken over as head coach of the University of Virginia. He also added that he recommended me very highly to Voris and that I would be hearing from him. The next day, Voris called and offered me a job as an assistant on his staff. It was an odd beginning. Without having met Voris personally and without ever seeing the University of Virginia, I accepted his offer. The pay wasn't much, $6,500. But at this point I wasn't in any bargaining position. After all, I had no record or previous experience as a coach. I was a player whose career was suddenly ended.

As it turned out, my first year of coaching was not a pleasant one. When I reached Virginia, I discovered that the scholastic standards were so high that it was not only tough to get a player in school but also once you did, it was tough keeping him in. I did enjoy the coaching end of it, however. We had a small staff but we had numerous meetings and exchanged a great many ideas. Voris was well organized. All of the assistants contributed in putting together our first playbook. I thoroughly enjoyed that part of it. But I have to admit that I was quite disappointed when I discovered that we were very lean as far as the athletes we had compared to the athletes we would be competing against.

I had first heard about playbooks as a member of the Cleveland Browns. Paul Brown's teams were ridiculed throughout the league because everywhere they traveled they always had notebooks under their arms. I'm sure the other teams had notes and plays written down, but they didn't carry the playbook with them all the time. Now everybody does it. Nothing is left to chance. The playbook has everybody's assignment for every play. A portion of the playbook is also set aside for individual positions. The halfback, for example, would have all the things that pertained to his position, the quarterback all the things that pertained to his position, and so on. But it would all be in the framework of what everybody does on each play. The players start memorizing this right at the beginning of training camp, and then each night we review a section in the classroom and then go get it done on the field.

The playbook really is a bible for everything that you are going to do either offensively or defensively. The playbook also talks about specific techniques such as run-offense, pass-offense, details of each assignment —if you are an offensive lineman, pass blocking techniques that you want to use for your quarterback, the outline of the quarterback fundamental. If you are a defensive back, back-peddling and drills used for defensive backs. It has everything in there that you want to accomplish in your training camp and as you prepare for the regular season. And then what you do each week is to take from this playbook and try to narrow down the things that you want to use in the ball game against the team you're playing, because of the tendencies that they show offensively and defensively.

We worked hard on fundamentals in spring practice and got to the point where we started the fall with a fairly decent first team. We lost our first game to Clemson but then upset Duke, which was heavily favored to beat us, the following week. The staff felt pretty good about things. In our third game against North Carolina State, our quarterback was injured seriously and was lost for the season. Although the game was close, we lost and from then on we had trouble competing. We just didn't have any depth. We finished with only that one victory against Duke, and the apathy of the students was evident. They only attended the games they considered important and mostly we were playing to half-empty stadiums. The college spirit wasn't anything like I thought it would be.

I was sharing an apartment with another coach and one night I was alone just staring up at the ceiling wondering just what direction my life was going to take. The more I thought about it, the more I realized that I was now in my life's work. Then I began to think about Dorothy. She was in far-off Hawaii and I was here. I began to realize that more and more I wanted her to become part of my life.

But what about Dorothy? Maybe her feelings had changed since she got to Hawaii. Maybe she had met someone else. It happens all the time. So I decided to write her a letter immediately. I don't know how many people wrote letters of proposal but I certainly was going to do it. Maybe Emily Post wouldn't agree. But at this point I couldn't care. I asked Dorothy to give up her teaching job when the semester was over and come back home so we could get married.

Dorothy has always been the most important person in my life. Whenever the big decisions had to be made we would sit down and discuss all aspects of the situation together and time after time she would always be there with the right answer. It was never, "How can I leave my friends, or the house?" but, "If you think it's the thing to do, let's do it." The fact that she is by nature an outgoing woman has also helped me get over my basic shyness.

Dorothy did write back and accept my proposal. We began making plans for our wedding date and what we would do afterward. Again this was all done through the mails. Now that I look back it does seem sort of strange. Here we were making the most important decisions a man and a woman could make at the time and we were writing back and forth like a couple of pen pals. It was the old cliché of absence makes the heart grow fonder that eventually got me to make a move toward marriage. When Dorothy was home and there were other girls to date, I just didn't feel any sense of urgency about settling down. Now that we were apart I wanted so very much to be with her.

What I had to do now was to settle my own coaching plans. While I really hadn't enjoyed my first year in coaching, I felt it was a year that I was fortunate to go through. It provided me with experience in handling young people. Instead of talking to them on the pro level, I had to talk to them on a teacher-pupil level. I couldn't assume anything and I would start teaching them right from the first step.

Long after the season I was still pretty disgusted. I knew I couldn't come back to Virginia. I attended the college coaching convention and was delighted to see Blanton Collier, my defensive backfield coach when I played with the Browns. Blanton was now head coach of the University of Kentucky. All his life he had been an assistant coach and now he had the opportunity of coaching at his state university. Blanton is probably the best teacher of technical football in the game and a superb organizer. We immediately began talking.

"What have you been doing, Don?"

"I just finished my first season as an assistant coach at Virginia."

"How did it go?"

"Fine in many ways. But I'm not too happy there."

"Would you be interested in working for me at Kentucky?"

"Do you have a spot for me?"

"I most certainly have."

"You've got yourself a coach."

In the next few weeks I made a trip to Kentucky. I met the rest of the staff and was quite impressed with the athletic setup they had. I also felt that the caliber of football in the Southeastern Conference was a lot tougher than at Virginia. After visiting Blanton, I decided I would very much want the opportunity to coach under him. There was also a good raise in pay that went with the job. I was making $6,500 at Virginia and I would be getting $7,500 at Kentucky. I would also be given a house rent-free right on campus.

But, there were a few matters I had to take care of first.

Blanton believed in hard work and we spent a lot of time meeting in the basement of his home beside the offices. Everything was meticulously planned. It was refreshing to get back into such an organized setup. I was absorbing a lot of background for the responsibilities I was to encounter when I would get my first head coaching job. We had a highly qualified staff. There was Ermal Allen, who later went to the Dallas Cowboys; John North, who went to the Detroit Lions and is now with New Orleans; Howard Schnellenberger, who is now the head coach of the Baltimore Colts; and Bill Arnsparger, who is the assistant head coach of the Miami Dolphins.

Despite the brain trust we had a losing season that first year. The athletes from the state were good, but not good enough to compete against the teams in the conference. The state of Kentucky has only one hundred-some-odd schools playing football and an awful lot of recruiters canvassing the state. The players that Kentucky managed to get weren't enough to win consistently in such a tough conference. Yet, from the standpoint of background, this was the most influential year that I had in coaching.

Basketball was the big sport at Kentucky with Adolph Rupp at the helm. Rupp was a strict disciplinarian who made even Paul Brown look like an easygoing fellow.

Some opportunities began to pop in pro football. I first received a call from a Canadian team asking whether or not I'd be interested in coaching in Canada. I told them no. Later I got calls from the Chicago Cardinals and the Detroit Lions. Both teams were looking for a coach who was a former player and had coaching experience. I didn't want to rush into making any decision. The thought of coaching in the pros was so appealing that I had to at least pursue the offers. I scheduled a weekend trip to both Chicago to meet with Pop Ivy, the head coach of the Cardinals, and Detroit to get together with George Wilson, the head coach of the Lions. I had good interviews with both organizations. However, I was impressed with the setup at Detroit.

When I returned to Kentucky, I talked over the opportunities with Dorothy. I decided to accept the job with the Lions as the defensive backfield coach. The pay was good, too, $11,000. It represented more money in my third year of coaching than I ever made as a player. The most I ever received as a player was $9,700, and that was in my seventh season. So, I had to inform Blanton of my decision. He was very understanding and actually guided me.

"What are your long-range goals?"

"You mean as far as coaching is concerned?"

"Yes. What do you eventually want to be?"

"There's no question that I want to be a head coach in pro ball."

"Are you positive?"

"That has always been my desire even when I was a player."

"Well, if that is your ultimate goal, then there is no doubt that you have to take the job with Detroit."

I was happy to be back in pro ball. When I first walked into George Wilson's office, he gave me a defensive playbook that was used the season before and told me to learn to set it up the way that I wanted so that I felt comfortable teaching it.

I'll never forget the first play I was responsible for as a coach. I always sat up in the press box the first half observing the action. Then at half time I would go down to the dressing room and make the necessary corrections. In the second half, I would stay on the field and work with the defensive backs and linebackers. On the first play, we lined up on what we called one-coverage or single coverage. The Browns came out in a tight formation with Ray Renfro, a fine receiver, as the weakside end in tight. As Renfro lined up, I could see that our secondary was a little confused as to what the coverage was supposed to be. The ball was snapped and Renfro took off from the tight end position and broke to the inside. Milt Plum faded back and hit him with a perfectly thrown pass that went about sixty yards for a touchdown. I almost fell out of the press box.

We lost our first three games and were behind in our

fourth. But we turned things around, won the game, and played good football the rest of the season. The Lions finished second in the division and played in the Runner-Up Bowl in Miami. It was the first of three straight appearances for the team in that game. I was responsible for the linebackers and the defensive backs and for coordinating the defense. There was some feeling of accomplishment by playing in the Runner-Up Bowl, but it wasn't the feeling that I wanted and that's the ultimate feeling of winning the world championship.

I gained the valuable experience of working with older players, many of whom were much better players than I had been. Fortunately, I had a strong defensive leader in Joe Schmidt, who was the middle linebacker and defensive captain. Joe was easy to work with and his leadership was instrumental in making the Lions one of the great defensive teams. Night Train Lane was in one corner, Dick Le Beau in the other, Yale Lary was stationed at the free safety and Gary Lowe at the strong safety. Schmidt was the middle linebacker, Wayne Walker was the right linebacker, and Carl Brettschneider was the left linebacker—a very tough unit. The defensive front four was led by Alex Karras and Roger Brown at the tackles and Darris McCord and Bill Glass at the ends.

The coaching highlight of my three years with Detroit occurred one Thanksgiving Day against the Green Bay Packers. The Packers were the world champions and they were beating everybody. Their offense appeared unstoppable. They had such stars as Bart Starr,

Jim Taylor, Paul Hornung, Boyd Dowler, and Max McGee, an outstanding team. On this particular day, we demolished them. Practically every time that Starr set up to pass, he was swamped. Their runners never could turn up field. Our defense completely dominated the game. It was such a delight to the fans that when the offense took the field they actually booed. They wanted to see our defense play the entire game against the Packers. It was probably one of the greatest defensive performances of all time. The recognition I received from it as the defensive coach was very instrumental in my later getting recommendations as a head coach.

The three years under Wilson gave me another insight into the game, which has been a key factor in the way that my coaching personality has taken shape. Wilson was a man-to-man type of coach. He was a tough, hard-nosed player with the Chicago Bears and he dealt with his team like one player to another. George wanted to treat the players the way that he wanted to be treated as a coach. He gave them a free hand, yet he expected them to be ready to practice and to work hard to prepare for the games. It was much more of a hard-nosed approach compared to the Paul Brown teacher-pupil relationship. I could see a lot of values in the type of relationship Wilson had with his players.

Up until this point I had been exposed only to the Paul Brown school with a little college coaching thrown in. Coaching in college had taught me the value of teaching. I had to start from scratch with young players and take them step by step. When I got back to pro ball, I carried this philosophy with me. I left nothing to chance. If I had jumped from being a player to an assistant in pro ball, I would have been in serious trouble. I guess I didn't really understand what coaching was all about until I was in the college ranks working with youngsters coming out of high school. Coaching on the college level taught me the value of detail, the importance of explaining everything to the bare essentials, making sure the players weren't left in the dark.

The biggest influence on my coaching life has been Paul Brown. Paul believed in the businesslike approach. He emphasized classroom techniques in which he could expound on the five theories of learning as he called it. Paul believed that everything stemmed from learning. He said that you learn by seeing, hearing, writing, practicing, and reviewing. Every year after his opening remarks in training camp he would lecture on what he called "basic information." The first question he would ask is, "Why do we have a playbook?" However, instead of just passing out the answers and reviewing them with the players, he passed out blank pieces of paper.

I well remember the evenings we spent in meetings at training camp in Bowling Green writing down this basic information. It was tedious work. Paul would dictate and the players would write it down word for word. This was his way of making you learn by writing. As I looked around the room and saw players like Otto Graham, Mac Speedie, and Marion Motley doing the same thing, I realized the importance that Paul put in this method of teaching. Here were superstars who had been champions year in and year out doing the same thing that I was doing as a rookie: Why do we have a playbook? . . . form in running . . . how do you improve running? . . . fundamental position . . . why do we take this position? These were just all very basic things that could have easily been put into a playbook all mimeographed and passed out. But Paul believed in teaching this way.

When I became a head coach I deviated from Brown's method. We use many adaptations of Paul's ideas but mimeograph them instead of having the players write them down. This way the responsibility falls on the assistant coaches to go over the playbook with their men and establishes good communication. I feel you can get as much done this way by going over it and underlining important phrases or rules that you want to make certain the players understand.

Brown was stand-offish and aloof with his players. I felt that it was good for Paul to be that way. But I also felt that I had to do it my own way. My own personality had to emerge. I still pattern myself after the Paul Brown teacher-pupil relationship, but I like to establish the feeling with my players that they can talk to me anytime on any subject and I'll understand. The fact that I had been a player and always enjoyed good relationships with the team makes me more of a George Wilson type of coach as far as communication goes. I believe in approaching everything from the teacher standpoint but also believe in sitting down and rationalizing, talking and joking a little instead of making everything so serious.

If there is one word that I would like to think describes my relationship with the players, it's natural. I want them to be natural and talk to me without tension, to consider me not simply a coach or teacher who isn't able to warm up to them on a friendly or humorous basis. When you get down to it, it is the personality that emerges in everything that you do.

It's been that way ever since I was a kid. On the playground I was the one who was always interested in doing the organizing, making sure that the participants were divided evenly so that the competition was as equal as could be, and always playing by the rules and the regulations. Becoming a coach started right there in a playground in Painesville, Ohio. Cleveland, Baltimore, Washington, Charlottesville, Virginia, Lexington, Kentucky, and Detroit were merely stops along the way.

5

It was my big chance. I was only thirty-three years old and now I had an opportunity to become a head coach. I would be the youngest coach in the National Football League if I got the job. I wanted the job and the challenge. The extent of my experience in the NFL had been my three years as an assistant coach at Detroit. Now I was being recommended to take over as head coach of the Baltimore Colts. The Colts had been a championship team. Why would they take a chance on an unknown?

The Colts were in Detroit to play the Lions near the end of the 1962 season. The night before the game, I met with Carroll Rosenbloom, the owner of the Colts. I remember one of the questions he asked me, and although I didn't want to come on too strong, at the same time I wanted to appear confident.

"Are you ready to become a head coach?"

"The only way that you'll ever be able to find out is

to hire me and let me show you that I am capable of being a winner."

I left it at that. I had played with Baltimore as a defensive back. Some of the players that I played with were still active, Gino Marchetti, Bill Pellington, Joe Campanella and a few others. Rosenbloom had a great deal of respect for their recommendations. He was a type of owner who listened to the advice of his veteran players. He would seek it and then make his own evaluations. They were aware of the strong defensive teams that the Lions had over a three-year period, from 1960 to 1962.

In the next few weeks, Rosenbloom and I talked a great deal on the phone. We finally arranged to meet again, this time at the Golden Strand Hotel in Hollywood, Florida. When the meeting was over, Rosenbloom hired me. It was a great risk on Rosenbloom's part. I admired him greatly for having the guts to make the change. He had based his decision on the recommendations of some of the players and that of Don Kellett, his general manager. Kellett and I had known each other from my playing days with the Colts through the years I was an assistant coach at the University of Virginia, the University of Kentucky, and the three years I spent at Detroit.

The coach I replaced was Weeb Ewbank. He had led the Colts to consecutive world championships in 1958 and 1959. But since that time, the Colts had slipped. They became a .500 ball club, which in Baltimore wasn't acceptable. I knew immediately what my job was—to restore the Colts to the championship level they once had attained.

My first year, 1963, wasn't an especially successful one. It wasn't until the final game of the season that we were able to go over the .500 mark, finishing with an 8–6 record. Yet, it was a significant season. Until mid-season we were 3–5, but we won five of our next six games to finish strong. That was the thing that mattered. With a strong finish, we had shown progress.

During my first year, I used a lot of young players. I felt the Colts had gotten old in certain areas and I decided to go with the younger players who demonstrated talent. This was the big reason why we got off to such a slow start. However, we did establish the fact that we could win with a young team in the final six games, which was important for the future.

The future came in a hurry. The very next season we enjoyed a great campaign. We went on a tear, winning eleven games in a row, and finished with a 12–2 record. Some people even talked about this being one of the greatest teams ever. We were rudely awakened, however, in the 1964 championship game against Cleveland. Shocked to say the least. The Colts were strong favorites to defeat the Browns for the NFL title. After a scoreless first half, we completely fell apart. So much so that we were beaten 27–0. I was embarrassed. A fine season down the drain. Those are the things you remember.

We started out pretty strong in 1965. Then Johnny Unitas got hurt one week in a game against the Chicago Bears. He fell under the crunching force of a high-low tackle. Unitas injured his knee, was operated on immediately after the game, and was out for the season. Then Unitas's fine backup quarterback, Gary

Cuozzo, got hurt the following week against the Green Bay Packers. Cuozzo suffered a shoulder separation, was operated on the same night, and he, too, was lost for the rest of the year. I couldn't believe it. In two weeks I had lost two quarterbacks. The injuries couldn't have happened at a worse time. There was only one more game remaining on the schedule, but it was a big one, against the Los Angeles Rams in Los Angeles. It was a Saturday afternoon game, which meant we had one less day to prepare for the game—and without a quarterback.

The Los Angeles game was one we had to win. We were battling Green Bay for the Western Division crown. The Packers were a half game ahead of us. We had a 9-3-1 record as we approached the final game of the season. There were three alternatives riding on that final game, all based on whether we won. If the Packers won their final game, they would win the title regardless. However, if they lost, then we would be the champions. If they tied, then we would have to play them in a special playoff game to determine who would represent the Western Division against the Eastern Division in the NFL championship game.

That week was one of the strangest weeks of coaching I have ever experienced. On Monday morning Art Rooney, the owner of the Pittsburgh Steelers, called. He knew the quandary I was in and volunteered to help. He informed me that I could have his veteran quarterback Ed Brown if he could clear waivers. I thanked him and said I would welcome someone with Brown's experience. After all, we had no other quarterbacks on the roster. What if Brown didn't clear waivers? What would I do then? I couldn't wait to find out. I checked our personnel. The only two players I had with any quarterback experience were Tom Matte, a running back, and Bob Boyd, a defensive back, good athletes but players who hadn't thought about the position in four or five years. Adding to our troubles was the fact that neither one was a drop-back passer in college. Both had been basically roll-out quarterbacks who either ran or handed off the ball. Our system required a drop-back passer. Our whole offense was geared around it.

Still, I had to make a decision before the squad reported for practice on Tuesday. I decided that Matte would be the best choice. He was a running back and knew our offense. There really wasn't much time for learning with the Rams game on Saturday. I was just hoping that Matte could execute. That Monday evening I called Matte at home and told him that beginning tomorrow he would be the quarterback.

I could see that the squad's spirits were low at our meeting on Tuesday morning. I had to make them realize that this wasn't the end. We had another game and we would win if we all pulled together. I stressed that the defense could win the game for us. They could get us good field position and then we could beat the Rams with field goals. All the players were thinking that it was an impossible task without a high-powered offense. But I had to get their spirits up. It took a humorous incident to do it.

After the meeting we went on the field for a light

workout. Matte handled the offense and called a play in the huddle. The players broke and lined up. Matte began to call the signals. All of a sudden, without warning, the defensive linemen got up at the same time, as if on cue, and began to break out in laughter. I was amazed. What had them laughing was Matte's high-pitched voice. It loosened everybody up and we all had a laugh.

Later in the afternoon Woody Hayes, who coached Matte at Ohio State, telephoned me.

"You definitely going to use Tom at quarterback?"

"Yes I am."

"Well that's fine. You don't have anthing to worry about. Matte is a fine athlete. He can get the job done."

"That's great to hear."

"Well, I just wanted to call to assure you that Matte can play quarterback."

"I really appreciate the call. But I'm still worried, what with the situation the way it is, the final game of the year and only four days to get ready for it."

"I'll tell you one thing. Matte can make the big play no matter how tough the circumstances. He's made the big plays for me over the years. Oh, one more thing."

"What's that?"

"Matte has only one fault."

"He does?"

"Yes. His only fault as a T-formation quarterback is his inability to get the snap from center."

That's all I had to hear. A T-formation quarterback

who couldn't handle the snap count. My hopes at that moment rested on Ed Brown. I was hoping he would clear waivers so that he could report to us and begin getting ready. I received more upsetting news later in the day when Brown was claimed by another team. Now time was needed by either Pittsburgh or Baltimore to contact the claiming club and ask them to reconsider and withdraw the claim. There were no assurances that this would happen. At any rate, this would create a further delay. I had to plan on Matte as the quarterback even though Brown was the ideal pocket passer.

In most cases the Colts used as many as twelve sets of pass formations. It would be futile to expect Matte to learn that many; three would be adequate. He could learn them easily, and by the same token the three would be enough to keep the Rams' defense busy. I gave Matte eight plays to work off these formations, four runs, two pass, one screen, and one draw. Since he was such a good runner, Matte himself could keep the Rams off balance by occasionally faking a hand-off and run the ball himself. Matte also was given a wristband with the plays written on it. The wristband is now in the Hall of Fame.

The practices the remainder of the week weren't too good. In fact, they were awful. We practically looked like a high school team. There was confusion, uncertainty, and poor execution. The only refreshing note was Matte's high-pitched voice. Even though Matte had a history of ulcers, I felt as if I was the one who had them. Matte seemed unperturbed by it all. He never quit. When something went wrong, he just picked up where he left off and tried again.

After our workout on Wednesday, we left for Los Angeles, pinning our hopes on two slim factors. One was that Matte had the offense working pretty good by the last afternoon of practice. The execution was better than the day before and the new quarterback-keep plays that we had put into the offense for Matte looked effective. The other good news was that Ed Brown had cleared waivers. He was scheduled to report to us the next day in Los Angeles. As late as it was, I was still happy to have him. I didn't know how much he could help, just two days before a game, but at least he was an experienced quarterback who could throw the ball. As soon as Brown reported, he was rushed to my suite for a cram course. Dick Szymanski, the center, and a couple of assistant coaches were on hand to instruct Brown. He was given fewer plays than Matte to learn.

That afternoon, both Matte and Brown worked out with the offense. Brown's cram course in the hotel helped out. He knew what he was doing out there and it gave the squad some confidence. The day before a game we usually devote to a light workout with the emphasis on the kicking game. But because of the predicament we were in, we once again concentrated on our offense, with Matte and Brown taking turns. The players appeared looser than they had been all week and I felt a little better about our chances against the Rams. That night, Rosenbloom took the entire squad to dinner at one of the finest restaurants in Los Angeles. I was in a good mood and so was the rest of the squad. However, just a short time later, we had another set-back. I was told that Matte remained at the hotel because of a fever and the possibility of coming down with the flu.

At the pre-game meal on Saturday morning, I talked to Matte. He looked drawn but assured me that he was all right. We looked horrible in our pre-game practice at the Coliseum. Everyone appeared flat. There was no chatter among the players. Matte couldn't complete a pass. Brown, too, was missing. It was unbelievable.

In my pre-game speech, I urged the team to get on that field and beat the Rams. I told them that this was the biggest test of their lives as players. They were facing tremendous adversity, playing a crucial game without Unitas and Cuozzo. It would be easy to give up. No one would criticize them for their efforts in view of the odds they faced. But, if they rose above the adversity, they would be praised by everyone for a great team effort. I told them they could win the game. I said that the defense would win it for us. They could stop the Rams and we could score enough points to win. There was no reason they couldn't upset the Rams if they wanted to. They had to be proud enough to do it.

I didn't know what to expect. Certainly the odds were against us. But everyone seemed to pull together, the defense and the offense. At half time, we were ahead, 10–7. I was proud of the way they played and I told them so in the dressing room. All they had to do was to keep playing inspired football and we'd end up winning. The Rams scored a touchdown in the third period and went in front, 14–10. Even though we didn't do anything on offense in the period, our defense had kept us in the game. There was still one more quarter to play. Amazingly enough, Brown got us ahead. He was sent into the game with instructions to throw a pass up the middle to tight end John Mackey. He did and Mackey went sixty-eight yards for a touchdown that gave us a 17–14 lead. Matte then kept the Rams off balance with his keeper plays and Lou Michaels kicked a field goal to provide us with a 20–14 victory. We had accomplished a fantastic victory against insurmountable odds. What a feeling of accomplishment.

The triumph earned us a shot at the Western championship. Green Bay was held to a tie in its final game and we both finished the season with identical 10–3–1 records. The playoff game was scheduled to be played in Green Bay the following week. Matte, the instant quarterback, lifted our morale for the playoff game against the Packers.

Our performance that day against the Packers, again against the odds, was inspirational. The only sad part was that we lost, 17–14, in overtime. We lost on a disputed field goal, one which would have provided us with the victory. Near the end of the game, Don Chandler kicked a field goal that appeared to be wide. However, the officials ruled that the kick was good. Everybody on our team was in an uproar. The game films later revealed we were right. That hurt all the more. As a result the league then decided to raise the outside bars of the goal posts to make it easier for officials to determine whether a kick was good or not. These changes in goal post dimensions were referred to as the Baltimore Extensions. Another rule change was also provoked by that call. Instead of one official stationed underneath the goal post, the league decided to have two. One under the bar and the other behind it. This provided the officials with a better view of a kick, to determine whether it went inside or outside the post. That was one of the good things that resulted in the defeat—better conditions to judge the important field goal attempts.

After the loss I was asked one of the toughest questions that I have ever been faced with as a coach. Many of us had tears in our eyes because of the disappointment suffered in the loss. Yet, the first question I was asked by a reporter at the press conference caused me to lose my poise. He wanted to know whether or not I was thinking about my trip with the Colts to Miami to play Dallas in the Playoff Bowl. I couldn't imagine a newspaperman, after the tremendous effort that our team had made, asking me a question like that, knowing the way I felt. I was fit to be tied. I'll never forget it. It was one of the very few times that I ever lost my patience with a writer.

In the following months, I thought about the squad and how proud I was of their efforts. They had played two tremendous games against two of the toughest teams in the NFL and we had nothing to be ashamed of. With Unitas back, I looked optimistically to the 1966 season. However, although it was a winning season, 9–5, we didn't win any championships. To my way of thinking, it was a disappointing campaign. My ultimate goal is winning, and by that I mean winning all the way, a championship. That is the way I coach and that is what I teach. After a 12–2 record and a 10–3–1 one, the squad didn't progress, not with a 9–5 one.

The 1967 season was a strange one. After thirteen weeks of play, we were undefeated. We had an 11–0–2 record and found ourselves in another crucial game against the Rams in the final game of the season. The Rams were 10–1–2. However, if we lost, the Rams would be the champions of the Western Division, even though our records would be identical. Because of a point difference in a game that we played against each other, they would earn the right to represent the West in the world championship. Winning would give us an undefeated season, a fantastic accomplishment, while losing would put us in second place. We again suffered the pains of disappointment. The Rams won easily. They exerted a great amount of pressure on Unitas and he had trouble throwing the ball. So, in spite of an 11–1–2 record, we were again disappointed losers.

Once more I looked to the following season. Once more I wanted to face the challenge of winning a championship. I figured 1968 would be the year. However, we suffered a setback in training camp. Unitas came up with an elbow injury and at first we didn't think it was serious. But it became more troublesome and Unitas couldn't throw effectively. I had to get a quarterback. I called the Giants. They had Fran Tarkenton as their No. 1 quarterback and I figured that perhaps Earl Morrall would be expendable. The Giants were willing to give up Morrall for our No. 4 draft choice in the 1969 college draft. I agreed. However, the Giants changed their minds. Instead of a draft choice, they decided they would rather have Butch Wilson, a reserve tight end. I said okay. Wilson was traded for Morrall and it had to be the best trade that I've ever made as a head coach.

There were only a few weeks remaining when Morrall reported to camp. But, he grasped matters in a hurry, even though he had a completely new system to learn. He had always been exposed to systems that were exactly opposite in terminology to what we had in Baltimore. He had an enormous amount of adjusting to do, but he did it because of his great poise and intelligence. Morrall was simply fantastic. He led our team to more wins in one year than any other football team had ever won. We finished the regular season with a 13–1 record. He continued to win in the playoffs, first beating Minnesota and then the Cleveland Browns for the National Football League championship and the right to play in the Super Bowl. The championship victory over the Browns was especially satisfying to me. In 1964, they had embarrassed us, 27–0. We had tremendous execution this time and whipped Cleveland 34–0. Later I was told that my mother, who was sixty-eight years old at the time, was standing during the final minutes of the game screaming at the top of her voice: "Get one more touchdown! One more touchdown! We want to beat the Browns worse than they beat us."

There was great jubilation in the dressing room. We had won the National Football League championship. Now we had the opportunity to win it all . . . to beat the New York Jets in Super Bowl III. It didn't seem as if it would be difficult.

6

Johnny Unitas didn't agree with my decision to start
Earl Morrall in the 1969 Super Bowl against the New
York Jets. I may listen to the opinions of some players
but when a decision has to be made, I'm the one who
makes it. I had no qualms about starting Morrall. He
had a great year, leading us to fifteen victories, which
was more than any quarterback had ever won. He had
been voted the player of the year and had the full confidence of the squad. Against difficult conditions, reporting to the Colts and learning a completely new
system, he had done more than anyone could have
imagined. Morrall most definitely was the starting
quarterback. Besides, I didn't feel that Unitas was a
hundred percent physically. So I really didn't have that
big of a decision to make. I was quite satisfied with
Morrall.

During the course of the season, while we were winning with Earl and John was healing, Unitas was ques-

tioned time and time again about why he wasn't playing. His standard answer to reporters was cold, "Why
don't you ask the Man." That may have made it seem
that we had a strange relationship. But that's not so.
It's just John's way. I always felt that although we
were never close I had a good, honest relationship with
John. Becoming close to Unitas is something that only
a few people have succeeded in doing. I have always
respected John as a quarterback. When I got to know
John, I respected him as a person, although he was a
loner in every sense of the word. He, at times, was
friendly and concerned and interested in my thoughts
as coach. Only a few times did we ever exchange dis-
agreeable words.

When things didn't please him, he showed it. One
incident took place in a game against Green Bay where
we felt we knew the defensive signals the Packers were
sending in from the sidelines. The only time they were
of value, however, was when the Packers were going to
blitz. If we got the blitz sign, I would signal to an offensive tackle who would say "blitz" in the huddle and
Unitas would call a play that gave us maximum protection on a one-on-one pass with one of our outside receivers, either Raymond Berry or Jimmy Orr. On one
play I got the signal for a blitz and sent in the sign to
the tackle who relayed it to Unitas. As it turned out,
the Packers didn't blitz. I don't know whether they
felt we had the signal and were doing something to
counteract that or whether we didn't read the signal
properly. At any rate, instead of having a one-on-one
situation, we found that they were doubling up on the

THE WINNING EDGE | 101

wide intended receiver and the pass was knocked
down. After the play, Unitas glared at me on the sideline and kicked the dirt as he came off the field. I got
upset.

"Listen," I said, "it wasn't my fault. They crossed
us up and I blew it by sending in the wrong sign."

"Unless you're sure of what you're doing," Unitas
snapped back, don't interrupt my play calling."

As we approached Super Bowl time, John felt that
he was now ready to go and that he deserved the
chance to start because of his contribution to the Colts
in previous years and previous championship games.
He was disappointed when I told him that I was staying with Morrall. There was no reason to relegate Morrall to a reserve role. He didn't show any signs of
weakening. In fact, he looked stronger than ever in the
34–0 romp over Cleveland in the championship game.
The Colts played a perfect blend of offense and defense, with real machinelike execution. Even Rosenbloom was thrilled with the performance. He was interviewed on national television and said that he
thought this was one of the greatest football teams he
had ever seen. He also said that he thought I was the
best coach in professional football and that this had to
be one of the finest coaching jobs in history, winning as
we did without John Unitas. He said he hoped that as
long as he lived and that as long as he owned the Baltimore Colts, he would never have to look for another
coach. There was a lot of warmth in his voice and
there wasn't any reason why I should doubt his sincer-
ity. It was a tremendous moment and I was touched by

Rosenbloom's speech. At that moment I couldn't possibly envision the day we wouldn't be together.

We were heavy favorites to defeat the Jets. There were two factors that established this: the first was our 15–1 record and the second was the lack of respect for the American Football League by people outside it. Our squad was certainly confident. If anything, I had to be wary of any signs of overconfidence. League rules dictated that we had to be in Miami a week before the game. It was my first experience with this procedure. In a way, we were strict with the players. We had certain rules and regulations that they had to live up to. One was an eleven o'clock curfew. They were upset, feeling that they should be given more leeway.

During all of the time we were in Miami, there was the feeling that the AFL and its representative, the New York Jets, weren't qualified to play us in a Super Bowl and that it shouldn't be much of a game at all. Being heavy favorites didn't help matters. We were listed to win by anywhere from seventeen points to three touchdowns. That's overwhelming odds for a championship game. Another thing that contributed to our possible overconfidence was looking at films of the Jets. We didn't think they were really impressive. Their defense seemed awfully weak. It was tough showing these films to your squad and not having them get overconfident.

The thing I tried to point out, but it evidently didn't sink in, was that Joe Namath was a great passer. He had played with the same set of receivers over a period of four years. I think that Namath is the best pure passer in the game. He is intense on the field and he prepares himself well as evidenced by the way he executes. He's got a lot of Unitas in him in that he has tremendous confidence in his own ability and will stay in the pocket until the last possible second, risking bodily harm in an attempt to give his receiver time to get open. These are his long suits. Through the years Namath has demonstrated that he is very important to professional football. He certainly is colorful. The reason I admire him so much is that he's a tremendous competitor who plays hurt and still manages to stay in there and get the job done. I know he's been criticized for his lifestyle. As far as I'm concerned, his personal life is his own as long as he meets the club rules. I feel that way about my own players, too. Prior to the Super Bowl, Namath had made the remark that there were five better quarterbacks in the AFL than Morrall. He has a flare for this sort of thing. Morrall didn't get excited about the statement, but I think his pride was hurt a little that a rival quarterback from an upstart league had the audacity to say something like that. He was determined that he would play a good game and make Namath eat his words.

It was tough to concentrate on preparing for the game. There were so many distractions. It was almost a carnival atmosphere. The whole thing was very poorly controlled. There was a lot of time spent in the lobby of the hotel signing autographs. Then the press conferences with reporters. And then the reporters continually calling your room. It was just so unreal. We had to take a bus and travel through heavy traffic every day to Boca Raton to practice at St. Andrew's School, which was the Dolphins's training site.

I couldn't wait for Sunday, game day. Then it would be all over. It was one of the most unpleasant weeks I've ever spent in getting a team prepared to play a game. However, we were all still confident. Rosenbloom had scheduled a victory party at his house in Golden Beach. Before the game, we walked around the field at the Orange Bowl, as we generally do on occasion before a game, talking over last minute problems, last minute ideas I feel the owner might be interested in. As we did so, we came across Jets's coach Weeb Ewbank and went over to say hello as a matter of courtesy. During the course of our conversation, Rosenbloom asked Ewbank to come to his party that night. Ewbank looked at him, didn't say a word, and turned away. I was later told that Ewbank related this incident in his pre-game pep talk to his squad. Weeb's final remark to his team was: "Let's have a victory party of our own."

Actually, we played well in the first half. We had a lot of scoring opportunities but didn't take advantage of them. Our receivers dropped some passes that could have resulted in big gains. The most controversial play in the game was a flea-flicker, which we used in the first half. Morrall handed off to Matte who threw the ball back to Earl. Morrall then looked downfield to throw the ball to Orr. It was a certain touchdown. Orr was wide open in the end zone, frantically waving his arms. But Morrall never saw him. Instead, he tried to throw a pass to Jerry Hill coming out of the backfield, and the Jets intercepted. The Jets made a big play, one that cost us a chance to get on the scoreboard.

Despite the fact that we were behind 7–0 at half time, I decided to stay with Morrall. I felt that some of the things that happened to us in the first half of play were not Earl's fault. At the start of the second half Matte got us going with a long run that put us into Jet territory. It appeared certain that we were ready to make our move now. However, Matte fumbled on the next play and the Jets recovered. They capitalized on the opportunity for a score. After we got the ball back, I gave Morrall one more series to see if he could get us going. He didn't. When he returned to the bench, I told Unitas to warm up, that he would be going in on the next series of downs.

Unitas tried, but it was too late. He did manage to move us and scored a touchdown near the end. But it was not enough. The impossible had happened—the Jets won, 16–7. They played inspired football. Namath did an outstanding job of quarterbacking. Everybody had respected Joe as a quarterback before the game, but I don't think that anybody realized how good he really was until after his performance in the Super Bowl. He received a lot of credit for winning the game and deservedly so, but there many other factors too: the great defense played by the Jets, particularly in the second half; the tremendous running of Matt Snell, who put together one of the finest games a fullback has ever played; wide receiver George Sauer repeatedly beating our cornerbacks on patterns; Namath reading the blitz, throwing the football on the quick slant in pattern that nullified our blitzing tendencies. Yet, I think you have to give Namath the majority of credit. In the weeks prior to the Super Bowl, his actions and his leadership made the rest of the team feel they were capable of winning. The way he led them on the field gave them additional confidence. I think this is what really put the game away as far as the Jets were concerned. I can't begin to detail our disappointment afterward. It was like a death knell. This was the first time that a National Football League team lost to an American Football League team. Nobody will ever forget that. It will be written in the record books as such.

There would be a party all right, but it would be more like a wake. Hardly a word was spoken on the bus back to the hotel. The players just stared out the windows or straight ahead with looks of total disbelief. Sitting dejectedly in our rooms at the hotel, we were shook by screams in the hall. I looked out the door and saw Rich Volk's wife screaming, yelling for help. I couldn't imagine what was wrong. Volk, a fine safety, had been hit twice in the head during the game. Both times he had to come off the field. The first time he was hit, we kept him out of the game. Later, the doctor said that it was okay for him to play. He returned to action and got hit a second time. We took him out and he didn't play the rest of the game.

When I reached Volk's room I asked his wife what was wrong. She said that her husband had gone into convulsions. Fortunately, the doctor was nearby. We assisted him in holding Rick down in the bathtub while the doctor kept him from swallowing his tongue. He was then taken to a hospital in North Miami. For awhile, it was touch and go.

It was the darkest day of my coaching career—the earthshaking loss to the Jets together with one of my players almost dying. It was a day and an evening I'll never forget. I didn't feel much like going to a party at this point. But my wife and I went and managed to get through the evening as best we could.

Rosenbloom obviously understood how I felt and what a bitter loss it was for me to swallow. I also realized how tough it was for him to take. There couldn't be any joy in the defeat. It turned out to be a evening more or less spent consoling each other. When I spoke to the players, I told them that the only thing that we could do was to hope and pray that we were men enough to stand the test that was going to be thrown at us in the months ahead; to look a person in the eye and say, yes, we did blow it, but there is nothing we can do about it now except work toward getting another opportunity.

I found little consolation in my own words. The loss was bigger than anyone could imagine. It really strained the relationship between Carroll Rosenbloom, the owner, and Don Shula, the coach. Rosenbloom felt that he had let the entire National Football League down, having been the first owner to have a team lose to the upstart American Football League. It was something tough for a proud man such as Carroll Rosenbloom to swallow. It was also tough on Don Shula.

7

I felt a certain uneasiness returning to Baltimore following the Super Bowl loss. I knew that it would take a long time for Rosenbloom to forget. The loss would gnaw at him. He is an intense man, a proud person who likes to win. He loves the spirit of competition and the satisfaction of victory. I quickly found out just how much. A few weeks after the game, Larry Harris of the Baltimore *Sun* wrote a column in which he quoted Rosenbloom. It was the first indication I had of any dissatisfaction by Rosenbloom with my work. The essence of the column was that Rosenbloom was no longer "big on coaches." He felt they got too much credit when they won, too much blame when they lost. The column was distinctly negative. I received a number of telephone calls about the column and there was a great deal of comment about Rosenbloom's apparent dissatisfaction. I decided to talk to him and called him one evening. He was quite incensed that I brought up the subject of the newspaper column. He snapped at me that he had a right to say or think whatever he wanted to and that he was bitterly disappointed in our loss to the Jets in the Super Bowl. It was obvious to me then that our relationship was really beginning to deteriorate.

The defeat in the Super Bowl carried into the 1969 season. The off-season was a total embarrassment. When training camp started, I felt that although we had some players who were getting old on our defensive team, it wasn't time to break up a winning combination. As matters turned out, we had some defeats early in the campaign, and coupling this with the continued sting of the Super Bowl loss, we again had to decide whether to go along with the veteran players who had won the year before or make wholesale changes. I decided to make the changes. I moved Mike Curtis from the outside to middle linebacker; I inserted Ted Hendricks into the line-up as a starting linebacker, replacing Don Shinnick; and I replaced Lenny Lyles at cornerback with a rookie, Tommy Maxwell. After these changes were made, the squad started to turn around to some degree. But it was a bit too late. We finished with an 8–5–1 record and missed getting into the play-offs. It turned out to be my worst season since my first year in Baltimore. After the season, Rosenbloom was asked what he thought about my coaching. He said he still thought that I was one of the better coaches in football but was very disappointed in the season. He added that he would continue with me but our football team had to get things turned around.

The next indication I had that Rosenbloom was unhappy was in his selection of a general manager. He decided to replace Harry Hulmes who was then an interim general manager. Hulmes was placed in that situation when Joe Campanella, a very close friend of mine and a very capable young man, died suddenly during a handball game. The untimely death ended his short tenure as the Colts's general manager. Hulmes, who had been the public relations director, was given the opportunity to succeed Campanella but Rosenbloom was never happy with his work. Rosenbloom wanted to hire Don Klosterman, who was the general manager of the Houston Oilers. I felt it was a good choice, but I doubted that Don would leave a seemingly good situation in Houston to come to Baltimore. Rosenbloom became upset with me when I made my feelings known.

"Don't you think that Klosterman would leave Houston to accept a job with Baltimore?"

"I really don't think so."

"Don't you feel the Baltimore job is a good one?"

"Certainly it is."

"Well, I think that I can get Klosterman to come."

It appeared to be a challenge to him. And he did get Klosterman. At the time the decision didn't seem like it would affect me one way or the other. I had worked with other general managers before and it never was a problem because I was pretty much given control of the football operation. I was coaching the Senior Bowl, in Mobile, Alabama, after the 1969 season when the announcement was made that Klosterman was joining the

Colts. I was told that he and Steve Rosenbloom, Carroll's son, would fly down to Mobile to see me and to talk about the way that they wanted to set things up.

Along with being the head coach, I was also a vice-president of the organization. When Klosterman was introduced at a press conference in Baltimore, quite naturally some questions were asked. One was directed to Steve Rosenbloom when he introduced Klosterman: "How are he and Shula going to get along and what are their responsibilities?"

In answering the question, Steve replied, "Of course we all know that the only reason Shula was made a vice-president is that we needed one more person around to sign checks."

I was highly disturbed at the remark. Maybe I was becoming too sensitive but the remark disturbed me. I knew that things were changing and now I might not be included in areas where I had once participated. When Klosterman and Steve Rosenbloom visited me in Mobile, I made my feelings known. Steve claimed that he meant the remark as a joke. Yet, he could understand why I was upset when I heard it. Now he wanted to make sure I understood that he had meant it as a joke and nothing else. In discussing the new setup, it became evident that they expected Klosterman to become more involved in decision making. Regarding trades and other responsibilities, it was felt that Klosterman should contribute. After they left, I could plainly see that major changes were taking place, and it was apparent that they knew what was going on but that I didn't.

When I returned to Baltimore after watching the 1970 Super Bowl game in New Orleans between Kansas City and Minnesota, I was called into the office for a meeting. The discussion centered around different responsibilities utilizing a working chart of the organization. It was mentioned that Klosterman would attend the league meetings, something that I had enjoyed doing since 1964. I was told that I would not go to the meetings anymore but would be kept abreast of the happenings by Klosterman. While we were all sitting together, I asked them once and for all to make their position clear regarding my responsibilities. I added that if I didn't like them, then I would have some decisions to make.

Steve then called his father on the phone. Carroll was in New York preparing to leave on a trip to the Orient. He explained to his father that he was sitting in an office with me and had told me what my responsibilities were, that I no longer would be included in the league meetings. Then he told him that I had said that I had some decisions to make . . that I wanted to know what my responsibilities would be. So Carroll asked to speak to me. He spent the first part of the conversation telling me I was ungrateful despite everything that he had done for me and telling me that if I had some decisions to make to go ahead and make them. It was almost one big continual tongue-lashing session between Carroll and myself. At the latter part of the conversation he did calm down. He remarked that even though I wouldn't be going to the league meetings, I could take Dorothy on a vacation at the club's expense and do whatever I felt I should. He made it clear that he wanted Klosterman and I to work together on trades. Klosterman would do some of the telephoning and I would do some of it, and then we would get together and discuss what we felt best for the club. In a sense, I felt that this was taking away some of the responsibility that I had had before. I also looked upon the fact that I wouldn't be attending the league meetings as another step backward as far as my relationship with the Colts was concerned.

Shortly after, I received a call from another team in the league inquiring as to my availability. It was one of the stronger franchises and they were looking for a head coach. The timing was perfect. We spoke two or three times in general terms. When it began to get serious, I felt I couldn't go on talking with them anymore unless there was something solid to offer. But in the final conversation with them, one of the executives of the club said that rather than pursue the talks any further, they were going to keep the coach they had for at least another year.

It was evident at the time of the league meetings that my relationship with Rosenbloom was reaching an awkward stage. Instead of being invited by Rosenbloom, I was ignored and left behind. I could see that his thoughts about me were not the same. It wasn't anything of the nature of an open feud, but nevertheless we were getting further and further apart personally.

I had nothing but fond memories of the years I spent in Baltimore and with Rosenbloom. But I felt it would never be the same again. My seven years were beautiful, happy times. It was now, at the end, that I was disenchanted. I got my start in Baltimore and it will always hold a special place in my life. I was a young coach then, very ambitious, very enthusiastic, and very quick-tempered. Being around some of the older players, who had been involved in championship games, helped me to know more about how players felt and how they prepared themselves for a game. That was important. Yet, because there were so many old pros, I feel that I assumed too many things and neglected some teaching that should have been done in the early stages of my coaching career. But I learned. I found out that even the great pros have to be reminded of what you expect of them every week. I discovered it was something they looked for and if you failed, then it was neglect. One of the big things I learned was never to assume anything. Always make sure that you give complete details in game plan and any specifics you want executed on the day of the game.

Another thing I learned was that everybody is watching you all of the time. The coach-player relationship is important. If you joke with one player, make sure you do it with others in a similar situation. Tom Matte had a great personality and laughed easily. There were times when I chewed him out as much or more than any player I have ever coached. Because of Matte's personality, almost invarably we would later treat it lightly. In dealing with other players, who might not react like Matte, you have to be aware of just who they are so that they don't remember that Shula ended up laughing with Matte and not with them.

Mike Curtis is an intense player. He gets so keyed up before a game that the best thing to do is stay away from him. He was also very sensitive to any open criticism in a meeting. The best way to handle Curtis was to take him aside and explain his errors privately. I'm very fond of Mike and really admire and respect him as a middle linebacker. He has to be without peer. His ability is fantastic.

Because of the tremendous personnel we had at Baltimore, I developed a great deal of confidence in what our team was capable of doing in the two minutes before the end of the half and the two minutes before the end of the game. This was mainly attributable to Unitas. His poise under pressure rubbed off on the other players and the coaching staff. You learned not to panic. The amount of plays you can get off in that two-minute period is incredible. Sometimes I thought Unitas would wait until the two-minute mark of the first half and then decide to fight the clock and put points on the board, then save the rest of the excitement for the two minutes before the end of the game. He has to be the greatest quarterback who ever played the game in those two-minute situations. His poise and leadership at that critical time of the game had a great deal of influence on my thinking. I developed patience and learned not to make mistakes, but to wait for the other team to, then to capitalize on their uneasiness and lack of poise to put the points on the scoreboard.

It was during my years at Baltimore that the special

teams became so important to professional football. We were the first club to name a captain of the special teams. Our kicking game was very important to us and we spent a lot of time on it. We praised the players on the kicking teams in front of the entire squad and showed films of the kicking game. We made the established stars—Unitas, Berry, Marchetti, Pellington—sit in on these meetings. Their remarks, "nice play so-and-so," were really appreciated by the players who were on the special teams. Including the entire team in these meetings made the special teams that much more of a team idea instead of making the players feel they were relegated to duty on the suicide squads. I thought they were so important that I named a captain of the special teams. Alex Hawkins, a second-string wide receiver, with just fair ability but possessing a great desire to compete, was the ideal player to be named captain. The first time that Hawkins went out on field along with Unitas and Marchetti, our offensive and defensive captains, a funny incident occurred. When Hawkins was introduced to the captains of the opposing team, one of the captains stuck out his hand and said: "Captain who?" From then on Hawkins was known as "Captain Who."

I still remembered the excellent relationship I had with Rosenbloom during those years. He was a fine owner. Our relationship extended to our families; we shared many good times together. I am grateful to Rosenbloom for giving me my start as a head coach. But now that tie had reached an end. I had to move on. Memories belong to the past.

8

A telephone call from Miami newsman Bill Braucher caught me by surprise. We had been classmates at John Carroll University. He was a highly respected sportswriter for *The Herald* and we managed to see each other from time to time. However, Bill's call was a very confidential one. What he asked startled me.

"Would you be interested in coming down to Miami as the head coach and also becoming involved in ownership?"

"Are you making me an offer?"

"Well, I have the authority to speak about it."

"In what way?"

"Your name came up yesterday in a meeting with Joe Robbie, who owns the Dolphins, and Ed Pope, the sports editor of *The Herald*. Robbie indicated that he wanted to make a coaching change and Pope volunteered your name. Robbie said that he would love to get you if you were available but that he couldn't contact you because of the league rules against tampering. So, Pope suggested that I contact you since we went to college together."

"So Robbie is aware of it, I mean your calling me."

"That's right."

"Well, before I think any more about it, tell Robbie I'll call him in the morning. I want to hear it from him that he has an offer to make."

The next day I telephoned Robbie.

"Are you aware that Bill Braucher called me last night?"

"Certainly I am."

"Is the ownership part correct?"

"It most certainly is."

"That makes the deal quite attractive."

"What are your contractual obligations with Baltimore?"

"I am in a revolving contract with the Colts, one that was for five years."

"How many years do you have remaining on your contract?"

"Three more."

"That wouldn't be a problem."

"Before I talk any further about this, I want to make sure that I have permission to do so. I'll talk to Steve Rosenbloom tomorrow about it."

"What about Carroll?"

"He's out of the country and isn't available."

"But you are interested?"

"I am interested in exploring the situation with you

further. But first I have to inform the Colts's management."

"I'll look forward to hearing from you when you do."

Steve Rosenbloom was in complete charge of the team. He had been made president of the organization only a couple of months before. Carroll said that he was going to turn over the team to Steve because he felt that his son was now ready to step in and do the job. Having the authority, Steve's permission or refusal would determine whether or not I could pursue my discussions with Robbie.

The next day I met with Steve. I informed him of my telephone conversation with Robbie. I explained to him the possibility of ownership. Steve said he understood that it was an advancement. He felt that the Colts would in no way stand in my way if it was a chance for personal advancement. He gave me permission to continue to talk with the Dolphins organization. I called Robbie back and told him that I had spoken with Steve and had received permission to talk with him. I also suggested to Joe that it would be a good idea for him to talk to Steve. He agreed.

The offer from the Dolphins excited me. At least I felt better about things. Now I had something to look forward to. It gave me a feeling of being wanted. On the surface, the offer was attractive. I just hoped that everything would turn out all right. It was an opportunity that not many coaches get. The ownership part was like a dream.

After another telephone call, I arranged to meet

Robbie at the Marriott Hotel in Washington. We talked cordially one evening for about three hours. I was quite impressed with Robbie. He is a quick thinker and has a very alert mind. He is a person of strong convictions. But what really impressed me was his sincere desire to bring Miami a championship. I realized he would go all out to do so. I immediately felt better about the possibilities of joining the Dolphins.

I asked Robbie whether he had made up his mind completely about his existing coach, George Wilson. I was quite close to Wilson. I had been one of George's assistants at Detroit and he had recommended me for the head coaching job at Baltimore. I liked both George and his wife, Claire, and I was concerned. I wanted to know the situation before I considered the job any further. Robbie disclosed that he was going to fire Wilson regardless of whether I took the job or not. He wanted to make a coaching change.

The next day my attorney, David Gordon, joined the meeting. There were numerous financial details and tax problems that had to be worked out. Robbie arranged for him to meet with Charlie Hogue of Price Waterhouse, who are the tax accountants for the Dolphins. David and I then told Robbie that we wanted to study his offer and would arrange another meeting with him very shortly.

The next meeting was scheduled in Miami. Dorothy accompanied me and my attorney on the trip. We were met at the airport by Robbie's wife, Liz, who took us to a posh private resort called the Jockey Club. Arrangements had been made for us to stay there since

Shula was a hard-nosed offensive and defensive back at John
Carroll University in Cleveland.

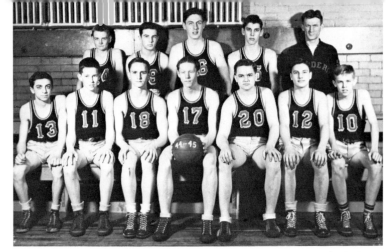

In high school, Shula was quite active in sports, particularly football, baseball, track and basketball. He is third from left in the front row (18), a laceration obvious on his right leg. The coach, Don Martin, was an early influence on Don's football career.

Shula's first coaching job was at the University of Virginia as an assistant. He was only 27 at the time, having played his final professional season with the Washington Redskins in 1957. The staff, from left: Bob Marish, Shula, head coach Dick Vooris, John Anastasia and Sam Timer.

Shula, at left, looks over notes with Norb Hecker during his last year as a player with the Washington Redskins in 1957.

Three happy faces at the University of Kentucky in 1959. Don was an assistant there under Blanton Collier, and his wife, Dorothy, and first child, David, approve.

OVERLEAF: Shula's first coaching job in professional football was as a defensive coach with the Detroit Lions in 1960. Clockwise, starting from top, Aldo Forte, head coach George Wilson, Bob Nussbaum, Scooter McLean, Les Bingaman, Shula and Larry Gersh.

In 1963, Shula became the youngest head coach in the National Football League at the age of 32 when he took over at Baltimore. At left is Colt linebacker Bill Pellington.

The happiness in Baltimore in 1964 was when the Colts won the Western Conference Championship. Assistant coach John Sandusky, right, embraces Shula.

The Colts enjoyed a European tour for the U.S. Air Force in 1965. From left, John Unitas, Shula, Gino Marchetti and John Sandusky.

Prior to the 1972 AFC championship game against Pittsburgh, Shula met with Steeler owner Art Rooney. Shula considers Rooney one of the finest owners in professional football.

Pre-game discussion involved Shula and New York Jet coach Weeb Ewbank. Shula played for Ewbank when he was head coach at Baltimore.

OVERLEAF: John Sandusky, who coached Baltimore in 1972, offers congratulations to Shula following the Dolphins' 16–0 victory over the Colts in the final game of the season.

Dolphin owner Joe Robbie presents Shula with a trophy symbolizing his 100th coaching victory. The milestone occurred during the
1972 season and in recording it, Shula became the first coach in
NFL history to win 100 games in his first 10 years.

In 1971, Shula was voted AFC Coach of the Year. He was presented with this trophy in the Orange Bowl in pre-game ceremonies during the 1972 season.

Coaching success has brought national fame to Shula. During a television commercial, he enjoys a laugh with some of his players. From left, Mercury Morris, Manny Fernandez and Norm Evans.

Prior to the 1973 Super Bowl, Shula and rival coach George Allen
of the Washington Redskins exchange thoughts.

During a time out, Shula discusses strategy with quarterback Earl Morrall.

Shula offers counsel to star running back Larry Csonka.

Hand on hip, Shula has a difference of opinion with a game official.

Waiting for the right moment, Shula rushes a player into the game.

A concerned Shula looks on as quarterback Bob Griese receives medical attention. Griese broke his right ankle during the fifth game of the 1972 season.

Shula addresses a press conference during the week before the 1973 Super Bowl in Los Angeles.

Anticipating victory in the closing seconds of the 1973 Super Bowl, assistant coach Bill Arnsparger warmly grabs Shula.

Players carry a happy Don Shula off the field on their shoulders following the Super Bowl win over the Washington Redskins.

The electric scoreboard at the Los Angeles Coliseum says it all after Super Bowl VII.

NFL commissioner Pete Rozelle presents the Vince Lombardi Trophy to Shula and Dolphin owner Joe Robbie after Miami defeated Washington, 14–7, in Super Bowl VII.

Dorothy Shula is as proud as any mother can be of her five children. From left, David, 14; Donna, 12; Michael, 8; Sharon, 11; and Anne, 9.

Dan and Mary Shula, seated, parents of Don, celebrated their 50th wedding anniversary in 1972. They were feted at a dinner when the Dolphins played a pre-season game in Cincinnati. Standing, from left, Don and Dorothy Shula; younger brother Jim; sister-in-law Dorothy; older brother Joe; sister Irene; brother-in-law Leonard Battista and sister Jane. (Sister Jeannette not pictured.)

The oldest of the Shula children is David, 14, who does chores around the football team.

There are many moods to Don Shula. He has a handsome, intense face that displays strength. He is a person of strong convictions. Often he is alone with his thoughts, which at times reflect tenseness, anticipation, worry, joy, concern, hope, relief. The many moods of Don Shula are channeled into one direction—winning.

our meeting wouldn't begin until the next day. Everything was being conducted in strict secrecy. After arriving at the club, we were whisked through the back door to our rooms. I had mentioned to Liz that we hadn't eaten on the plane and would like to have dinner. She suggested that we go down to the dining room since it was quiet and we wouldn't likely see any people that we knew.

So, Dorothy and I, joined by Gordon, went to have dinner. As we were escorted into the main dining room, the first person I spotted was Elinor Kaine, a sports columnist. I took a deep breath. She smiled and called me over to introduce me to several people in her party. During the course of conversation she said I'd never guess who was over at the bar having a drink. She then pointed at Vince Lombardi. A short while later Vince came over to our table. He was with Mike Manuche, a restaurant owner from New York. Naturally, he asked me what I was doing in Miami. I said we were down vacationing and left it at that. Imagine bumping into a writer and a rival coach at this time? Still, none of them linked me with the Dolphins. The only outside person who knew I was in Miami at the time was Steve Rosenbloom. I had kept him abreast of all my conversations with Robbie. In fact, he was in Miami at the same time, talking contract with Baltimore linebacker Ted Hendricks. I even tried to call Steve while I was in Miami but I wasn't able to get through to him. So, my visit to Miami was pretty much in secret.

The next day we met with Robbie and Pete Fay, the

club's attorney and now one of the Dolphins's owners. The meeting went well and we moved closer to finalizing and refining the many clauses in the contract. As I sat there, I kept thinking more and more to myself that I wanted the job. The opportunity and the challenge were there. Robbie appeared anxious for me to accept the terms that would make me head coach and part owner. It was the finest contract I had ever been offered. Still, there were a few points that had to be changed before it was acceptable to both parties.

The negotiations were reaching a point where Dorothy and I had to discuss the whole situation. I was perhaps one meeting away from signing. If I went ahead I would be uprooting my family's life once again. As she had in the past, Dorothy felt that whatever I thought was best for our family and for my work was also best for her.

When we returned to Baltimore, it was obvious that I had to take the offer for the opportunities it offered me and my family. Rosenbloom was still out of the country. I felt the sooner I told Carroll of my decision the better. There wouldn't be any purpose in sitting on it until he got back. Besides, if the story somehow leaked out it would be embarrassing for everybody.

I told Steve that I wanted to call his father. He told me to wait until Sunday, that Carroll was presently in Japan but would be in Honolulu then.

A few days later I placed a long-distance call and got through to Carroll. I disclosed to him that I had been talking with another team and had received permission from Steve to do so. I told him the offer they were making was an excellent one and I had pretty much decided that I was going to accept it. At the beginning, he was very kind and understanding. He said if I felt it was a move to better myself, then he wouldn't stand in my way. Then he asked me if I had talked to Rozelle. I told him I hadn't but I intended to. He then became less cordial. He turned very curt and very businesslike and said he wanted to call the commissioner and that I should talk to him also. I told Rosenbloom that I would have Robbie call him. The conversation ended quickly.

Feeling somewhat relieved, I called Joe. I told him that I had just finished talking to Rosenbloom and informed him that I was going to sign with the Dolphins. I suggested to Joe that he call Rosenbloom and he did. After he spoke with him, Robbie then telephoned Rozelle. Rosenbloom had stipulated over the phone to Klosterman that the Colts would release me from the remaining years of my contract if I agreed to three provisions. One, that I would not talk to any of the present Colt assistant coaches until a new head coach was named at Baltimore. Two, that I wouldn't take any materials that didn't belong to me from the Colts's office. And three, that any press release would have to be a joint one agreed upon by both organizations. I told Klosterman that the provisions were fair and reasonable and that I would certainly agree to all three of them.

The Dolphins were anxious to make the announcement. I had a final contract meeting scheduled with them on Wednesday and they were hoping they could announce the story that I was their new coach that night. On Tuesday night, I talked to Klosterman on the phone and we worked on the wording of the press release. The next morning, on the way to the airport, I stopped at the Colts's office. They had a release ready. I read it and made some changes. They accepted them and typed a new release. My attorney and I then left to catch a plane for Miami.

Once again we met at the Jockey Club. All the details of the contract were agreed upon. In the course of the discussions, Robbie placed a call to Rozelle. He informed him that I was ready to sign and to become head coach and part owner of the Miami Dolphins. Rozelle was informed that there was a strong possibility of the story leaking out since the Miami *Herald* had known about the negotiations. They were ready to break the story.

Robbie hurriedly arranged a meeting with George Wilson. He notified him that there was going to be a press conference in a few hours announcing a new coach. That night at the Jockey Club, the announcement was made to the news media.

In reality, everything happened so quickly, it was like sudden shock. I never imagined that I would leave Baltimore and wind up in Miami. I knew that Robbie had made overtures to Ara Parseghian of Notre Dame and Bear Bryant of Alabama before I was even considered. And, when I was approached about the job, I recalled meeting Joe only one time previously at a party after the Super Bowl. He introduced himself and his wife to me and we chatted for about a minute.

Now that it was over with, I could feel the tension in my body easing. My emotions over the past few weeks had been sky high and all I wanted to do was rest for a couple of days. But I knew I couldn't. There wasn't much time for that. There were too many things to do.

Shortly after the announcement was made that I was
the new coach and part owner of the Miami Dolphins,
the Colts accused the Dolphins of tampering. Tampering is a very serious accusation and the most disdained
act in professional football. It usually carried an extremely strong penalty. It was obvious that the Colts
were looking for some kind of remuneration. Their
complaint to Commissioner Pete Rozelle was that Robbie didn't ask the Colts's permission to speak to me.
Klosterman was quoted as saying that "in his opinion it
was tampering." He also felt that "this was handled in
a subversive manner." In pro football you are supposed
to follow protocol whenever you would like to hire an
individual from another football team. You first contact
the owner and ask permission to talk to the individual.
Ownership goes to ownership.

Shortly after Rosenbloom returned from Hawaii, the
accusations continued. They were beginning to hurt. I

was trying to settle down to the business of organizing a football team when Rosenbloom began to make his feelings known to reporters. Right after he named Don McCafferty to replace me at Baltimore, he appeared with announcer Joe Garagiola on NBC's "Monitor Open Line" and remarked "that I want a coach who wants to win and my feeling about a head coach is that he be one who must have rapport with his players, that he be fair at all times and, unfortunately, we have not had this since Weeb Ewbank left. I decided that Shula could do the job, and we brought him in and he has done a fine job, with the exception of winning the big ones. As you know, he left me with a legacy. I will always be remembered as the first NFL owner to lose the Super Bowl game. Shula did have rapport with his players but in the last couple of years that situation has changed."

Later he was quoted in print: "Everybody in the country knows that fellow Robbie was tampering when he took Shula away from us. They waited until I got out of the country to continue their little talks. Shula has very few fans among the players and I certainly am not one, either."

Bubba Smith made some remarks that hurt me, but the ones that hurt more than anything were by John Mackey. He claimed that I was two-faced and became a dictator in 1969 when the Colts didn't win. He remarked that I might have hampered the Colts's efficiency last year by making a puppet of quarterback John Unitas and that I panicked, as did the players, in the 1969 Super Bowl game against the Jets. He added that I thought I was the biggest thing since bubble gum and he wasn't sorry that I was gone.

Mackey's remarks didn't change my opinion of him as a player and a person. I've always had a high regard for both him and his family. When I left Baltimore I called him and thanked him for his contribution over the last seven years. I've always felt that any record I've had is attributed first to my assistants and then to the players. But you never really know what a player thinks of you until after you have gone.

In April, I received still another shock. Rozelle ruled that the Dolphins were guilty of tampering. As a penalty, he awarded the Dolphins's No. 1 draft choice in the 1971 college draft to Baltimore. I thought Rozelle's decision was unfair. He based his ruling on the manner in which the initial contact was made by the Dolphins. He felt that ownership should have first sought the permission of ownership before any contact was made. He emphasized that the Dolphins did not contact the Colts for permission to talk to me. Instead, it was leaked that there was a job available with ownership involved. When I received substantiation of the fact that ownership was involved, I then contacted Steve Rosenbloom and asked permission to talk to the Dolphins. Rozelle ruled this was wrong. If you look at the strict interpretation of the tampering rule, I guess it could be wrong. But I don't believe so in this case. I feel the Dolphins were victimized. There weren't any undercover dealings, secret meetings, or surprises to the Colts. I had informed them of the talks all along. Why, we even compiled the news release together after I decided to join the Dolphins. What bothered me was that there had been incidents of this nature that had gone on before that were not punished by taking away a first-draft choice. I thought it was harsh because it was a precedent-setting case.

Perhaps Rozelle was under great pressure from the owners. There were so many owners at the league meetings who were concerned about head coaches moving from one club to another with the inducement of ownership that they wanted to prevent repetitions. I believe this may have been why Rozelle took the action that he did. Professional football wouldn't be where it is today without a Pete Rozelle. In the early days of the sport, Bert Bell was a strong commissioner and the league couldn't have survived without him. But because of television, expansion, and the increasing popularity of the game, Rozelle was the ideal person to communicate with Madison Avenue.

Yet, I feel he could have shown more concern for me in dealing with the accusations Rosenbloom had made. When he finally did penalize Rosenbloom it should have been made public. Instead, Rozelle waited for a long period of time before revealing at a Miami press conference that he had fined Rosenbloom $5,000 for remarks against me. He later fined Rosenbloom for additional unfair and unjust remarks. When he fined him the second time I asked Rozelle if it was going to be made public. He said that he would much prefer to let it drift out by word of mouth and eventually it would be known by all the owners. When he announced that the Dolphins were guilty of tampering and penalized them their No. 1 draft choice, it made headlines all over the country. Yet, he felt that the fines inflicted on Rosenbloom should not be announced publicly. If they were, then they would have put a vastly different light on the things that Rosenbloom had said about me, which were picked up and printed in newspapers and national magazines as well as on television. Millions of people knew of Rosenbloom's accusations about me; yet they really never knew about the fines Rozelle levied on him.

Rozelle should have said publicly that I did not break my contract with the Baltimore Colts. That has been established as fact by him. I asked for and was given my release from my contract. The commissioner should have made that clear. Even now, *Sports Illustrated* and another national magazine all but said that I broke my contract with the Colts. Privately he has said that I acted in good faith and that he believed everything I said about the entire move from Baltimore to Miami. Why he hasn't defended me publicly, I don't know.

Rosenbloom later made the statement that my going to Miami saved him from having to fire me and that Miami was actually taking Don Shula off of his hands. I would have liked to have thought that when I left, I could go on my way without so much discontent. Rosenbloom would continue to operate his football team and just find somebody else to coach. But a lot of unpleasant things happened and I think that these should be known. But life goes on and I had to get a football team together.

Robbie had given me complete freedom with the football operation. He wanted a winner and I wanted to give him one. In the months ahead, I got to know Joe better. Before I met him, the only thing I knew about him I learned from a very unflattering article about him I had read in *Sports Illustrated*. I even gave it to my attorney and told him to read the article before we first met Robbie. Both Gordon and myself were convinced that Robbie was an honest person who wanted to do what was right. Everything was aboveboard in our contractual meetings. What he promised he has lived up to. We've had some misunderstandings but they've been minor ones. On the big issues, Joe has gone down the line with me and backed me in every way. I'm very happy with our relationship. He isn't at all the way *Sports Illustrated* made him to be. Robbie has always defended his position on the tampering issue. I admired the statement he made long afterward.

It never occurred to me either then or now that if a person under contract is told that he can discuss entering a new contract with someone else, the someone else needs permission to talk to the person under contract. Commissioner Rozelle agreed that Shula had obtained permission from the Baltimore Colts to talk to me, but he held that I needed permission to talk to Shula. Think about that for awhile. Shula could talk to me but I couldn't talk to him.

I chuckled at his answer to a fan who asked him if he was going to give me time to make the Dolphins a winner.

"He's got all summer," snapped Robbie.

What I had to do first was to assemble a coaching staff. In building a winning organization, it is essential to surround yourself with qualified assistants. The first coach I hired was Bill Arnsparger, who had resigned from the staff in Baltimore because of some personal problems. He also was offered a business opportunity that looked too good to turn down. After a great deal of thought, he decided that he would join the Dolphins. Bill is a solid individual who had been with me for six of the seven seasons in Baltimore. He was thoroughly familiar with the system I would be installing. I felt he would be ideal to take charge of the overall defense while working specifically with the linebackers.

Then I hired Howard Schnellenberger. He had been an assistant with the Los Angeles Rams under George Allen for four years. Previously, he was a top assistant under Bear Bryant at the University of Alabama. Schnellenberger was unhappy with the situation in Los Angeles. He had not signed his contract when he learned I was in the process of moving. He said that he was very interested in joining me at Miami. After a couple of phone calls, the deal was finalized. Right away I had two strong assistants. Arnsparger had been exposed to winning football at Baltimore for six years and Schnellenberger had the same exposure under Bryant and Allen. I made Schnellenberger the head offensive coach, who would be responsible for the offensive book. I also wanted him to work primarily with the receivers, something he had done at Alabama and with the Rams.

Next I signed Mike Scarry who had been a defensive

line coach with the Washington Redskins until Otto Graham was fired. At the time Scarry, who had time remaining on his contract, left coaching and was working as a personnel expert primarily connected with the San Francisco 49ers. I phoned Mike and learned he wanted to get back into coaching. What I liked about Scarry was that he was a winner as a player. He was the first captain of the Cleveland Browns. Although he was small, he played both ways, as an offensive center and as a linebacker. He was imbued with the winning tradition of the Browns.

Then I hired an old friend of mine, Carl Taseff. Carl's duties were chiefly with the offensive backs. He would also be responsible for scouting future opponents. Taseff, too, was involved with winning, in college and with the Browns and Colts.

The next person that I wanted to get was John Sandusky as my offensive line coach. He was a close personal friend who had been an excellent assistant in my years with the Colts. However, one of the conditions laid down by Rosenbloom when he agreed to release me from my contract was that I didn't approach any of the assistant coaches until a new head coach was hired. When Don McCafferty, who was also an assistant on my staff, was named as head coach, Sandusky decided to stay in Baltimore.

However, Monte Clark, who had played a number of years with the Cleveland Browns, indicated to some people that he was interested in retiring as a player and getting into coaching. I received two phone calls. One was from Chuck Noll, one of my former assistants, who is now the head coach of the Pittsburgh Steelers. The other was from Dick Nolan, the head coach of the San Francisco 49ers. Each recommended Clark. They both said he would make an exceptional coach because of the way he had prepared himself over the years. I got permission from Blanton Collier, who coached the Browns at the time, and owner Art Modell to talk to Clark. What I had heard was true. Clark said that he would accept a coaching position. So, I hired him over the phone even though he had no coaching experience whatsoever. It turned out to be one of the greatest moves I've ever made. When Clark reported to the Dolphins, he showed that he was eager, ambitious, and willing to work. Monte has been one of the key factors in the success of our running game—bringing some of the knowledge that he obtained as a player and helping us a great deal in putting our book together. He contributed a lot of ideas that were helpful in making our running game the best there is in professional football.

Rounding out the coaching staff was Tom Keane, who had been with George Wilson. Keane was a teammate of mine as a defensive back in Baltimore in the years that Taseff and I were there. I didn't know whether it was a good idea to keep a coach on the staff from the preceding regime, but I knew that Tom would work hard for me and decided to keep him. I completed my coaching assignments by placing Keane in charge of the defensive backfield.

My staff, carefully selected, was now complete. All of these men had at one time or another been associated with winning football, either as a coach or a player. They are the type of assistants I want around me—people who knew what it took to win and who were able to teach that kind of football. There would be a lot of hard work involved. It was a completely different picture, beginning in Baltimore and now starting again in Miami. During my years with the Colts, I had become a veteran coach and had developed winning teams and a winning record over a seven-year period. Now, at Miami, I was asked to take over a group of players who never had a winning season and had only a 3–10–1 record the year before.

The first thing was to learn as much as I could about the players, so I began with the analyses of Joe Thomas who was the player personnel director of the Dolphins at the time. Along with the rest of the coaches, we spent countless hours in the film room grading each player on each play from the year before. We looked at the individual skills of the players, trying to assess the raw individual ability of a player to either do his job or not do it. At this point we weren't concerned with comparing the types of systems they were exposed to or the techniques that they were taught. From this film study and statistical charting of the players we learned a great deal. We were able to determine the players who were getting the job done on the 1969 Dolphins and almost immediately to separate those from the ones who didn't have a chance for 1970. The hours studying films were well spent; we got to know the individual talents of each player before we got to training camp.

Bob Griese, Larry Csonka, Jim Kiick, Mercury Morris, Nick Buoniconti, and Dick Anderson were quite impressive. Norm Evans looked as if he was a player who was capable of excelling. We also could see the potential of Larry Little, although he didn't play much the year before because of a knee injury. Larry Seiple looked like a fine punter. The player that I felt had the most ability was Griese. He first made a tremendous impression on me when I was at Baltimore and played the Dolphins in a pre-season game in 1968. Griese was exceptional that night and we had trouble winning 22–13 because of the way he threw the ball. The next year we again played them in a pre-season game and Griese didn't look as good. Neither did the rest of the Dolphins for that matter. In fact, it looked to me as if they had gone a little backward instead of progressing in their development.

The most glaring weakness appeared to be the offensive line. It needed a great deal of work not only in execution but also in techniques. The defensive secondary seemed to sprout new holes in every game and had given up a great many touchdowns. Some of the weakness lay in what they were being asked to do. For example, there were a lot of single coverage situations, going one-on-one against some great receivers, and I don't care who you are, unless the execution is extraordinary, a great pass catcher is going to beat you with single coverage. The pass rush was weak and the opposing quarterbacks had a lot of time to throw the ball for big gainers and cheap touchdowns. When I evaluated the secondary, I knew I would have to make wholesale changes. The only defensive back who I figured to keep was Anderson and the only linebacker I would go with was Nick Buoniconti. I was going to have to gamble and go with new players in some key positions. It was a big risk, but it had to be done. On film, the Dolphins didn't show much.

I was proud of the winning percentage that we had produced in Baltimore, but if it meant throwing it out the window and sacrificing that to build this team, then that's what we would do.

Norm Van Brocklin, the coach of the Atlanta Falcons, always used to joke with me about being a push-button coach at Baltimore. He'd say that all I had to do was throw the ball out to Unitas and say, "Go win the ball game." Shortly after I accepted the offer to coach at Miami, Van Brocklin sent me a telegram. It read: "Congratulations on your first (and he underlined first) coaching job. Now you're going to know what the rest of us coaches have been going through all these years."

I had begun studying the personnel of the American Football Conference when Baltimore decided to move into the conference as part of the realignment dictated by the merger of the NFL and AFL. I didn't have a timetable for success. At my first press conference I said that I wasn't coming to Miami with a one-year plan, a three-year plan, a five-year plan, or a ten-year plan. That's not the way. I don't spend a lot of time trying to figure out what the future holds. The only thing I could guarantee was that I would work as hard and as long as possible to try and put the best team on the field.

Remember, the squad didn't know me and I didn't know them. My immediate objective was to bring the players to an indoctrination session in Miami. On April 25 I had my first contact with the players. I brought in both the rookies and the veterans and began to instruct them in our terminology and my way of thinking. The first meeting took place at the University of Miami and I outlined my objectives to a squad who didn't know what to expect of me. I told them that we would work with them as much as possible, especially the players who were living in the Miami area. As things turned out, we succeeded in getting a great deal accomplished with these players. We sometimes worked as much as two and three times a week at the University of Miami, going over terminology again and again, cadence, pass routes and such. It provided me with an excellent opportunity to work with Bob Griese and get him ready for training camp, which was scheduled to open early in July.

About this time I took another important step. We joined a scouting organization called BLESTO VIII. Robbie went along even though it cost the organization a good deal of money. He said that if this would help make us a winner, we should go ahead. We felt that we had to join BLESTO to compete. Joe Thomas was pretty much a one-man operation and the fear of something happening to Thomas made me decide that it would be best to have a backup scouting system. In joining BLESTO we felt that we were joining one of the best scouting organizations in football. The head of the group, Jack Butler, is someone who knows his business.

Taking away our No. 1 draft pick was a touch jolt to the team. When Rozelle's statement concerning tampering was printed in the newspaper it had a potent impact, especially among the Miami players. After all, what did they know except what they read in the newspapers? It made my move from Baltimore to Miami look that much more unscrupulous. I still was upset by it. I could see the puzzled looks on the faces of some of the players. I was a new coach to them and I had to immediately establish a trust between coach and player. So I told them not to judge me by what was said or what they read in the newspapers, but to judge me by how I treated them. This helped clear the air a bit but it certainly wasn't the ideal way to start off with a new team. If they reported to training camp distrusting me, then we would never get the necessary dedication that goes with winning. I wanted the air clear when the players came to camp.

The first training camp was that important. The close contact with the players living in Miami helped enormously. Some of the players were overweight and I asked them to report to camp in better condition. Larry Little and Larry Csonka were two prime examples. Checking them every week I could see that they would report in better shape. We also put a lot of the others on arduous weight programs, designed to build their strength. Others were placed on running programs to help them with their speed. The players were asked to do something extra and they were willing to do so. In the meantime, I made a couple of moves that may have appeared insignificant at the time but were designed to strengthen the club. I negotiated successfully for the rights to tight end Marv Fleming who had played out his option at Green Bay. I was successful in signing him. Then I was fortunate to sign another free agent, field goal kicker Garo Yepremian. With these additions and the attitude that the squad had displayed since I first met them in April, I couldn't wait for training camp to start to see just how much of a team I had.

But, my anticipation had to wait for a players' strike to be settled. Who would ever anticipate a players' strike? It was the first in the history of professional football and it left me fuming. My entire timetable was thrown for a loss. I had so much to accomplish in camp. Even then I could only hope that the prescribed time would be enough. I would have loved to plan on an additional couple of weeks. This was a whole new game and the players only ally would be time. Now, with the strike, instead of learning, they would begin by having to catch up.

The rookies, however, were unaffected by the strike and we gave them a good long look. We tried to conduct the camp as normally as possible, just as if the veterans were around. But it was hard working with the youngsters and thinking about the veterans and how much we could accomplish if they were around. Still, some of the kids began to make an impression. Mike Kolen, Doug Swift, Jake Scott, Tim Foley, and Curtis Johnson were getting extra attention and it turned out to be a break both for the youngsters and the club. The rookies had a great opportunity to display their skills and the coaching staff had the same opportunity to observe them. Something good came out of the strike after all—we discovered some talent that would contribute to the Dolphins's success. The kids got a foot in the door and pushed it open.

Finally, the veterans reported to camp on a Monday morning, just six days before our first scheduled preseason game against the Pittsburgh Steelers in Jacksonville.

The problem now facing me was getting the veteran players to catch up. Some of the younger players already knew more about the new system we had introduced than those veterans, who didn't work with us at the University of Miami. Under the regular two-a-day schedule it would be impossible to make up for lost time, so, I presented a plan to the squad that would make the most of every waking minute in order to get ready to play football. I told the players that we would have four-a-day workouts. Not two or possibly three, but four! They couldn't believe what I was asking them to do. Then I outlined the schedule: We would begin work at 7:00 in the morning and work on the special teams and the kicking game for half an hour to forty-five minutes. Then a break for breakfast. At 9:30 we would report for a half-hour meeting to go over the things we wanted to accomplish in the morning practice, which was devoted to the running game. The morning practice was an hour and a half in pads under a hot sun. Then a break for lunch until 3:00 P.M. to get together to discuss the afternoon practice. It was an hour and a half workout emphasizing the passing game, passer and receivers, pass protection and pass rush. We broke for dinner at 6:00, but were back on the field at 7:30 P.M. to work until dark, reviewing some of the things that happened during the day, making corrections and changes. Then time to shower and still another meeting at 9:30 for an hour. We again reviewed the events of the day and showed films of the practices. We had our own photographer taking films of the practices, so instead of a player trying to recall by memory some of the things that happened, we showed the films to pinpoint any mistakes that he had committed. It was an excellent teaching aid and it impressed the players because we showed them the extent to which we would go to get them ready to win.

Many of the players joked about the four-a-day practices. They said they felt more like strippers than ballplayers. They always seemed to be taking their clothes off and putting them back on. It was nice to have a laugh every now and then in view of the strenuous schedule they were asked to maintain. We kept the schedule all week. When we went to Jacksonville to play our first pre-season game, we even worked out that morning, also a radical departure. We won the game 16–10. The players were really impressed that we were capable of winning even though we had only been together for a week. The players gave me the game ball—it is something I'll always cherish because it came from a group of players who had been pushed harder than any other team had. In such a short period of time they not only were driven but also were tested and had met the test. That victory drove home the point of how hard they would have to work if they wanted to win.

The victory was the symbol they could point to for what I was asking them to do. I placed a great amount of emphasis on conditioning. As far as I am concerned, there is no end to it. It's the single most important factor that is needed to play a football game. Almost every team uses the Oklahoma Drill and I am sure it is nothing revolutionary or new. But it's something that I think is the essence of the game of football itself. It pits an offensive man, a blocker, against a defensive man and then a ball-carrier. And this is a situation you will always see as you watch a football game—a man with a football, a man out there blocking for him, and a defensive man coming in trying to make the play. That's where it's all at. We try to break down these elements in a drill to the bare essentials of football. In the Oklahoma Drill we take two dummies and set them about three yards apart. We'll take a quarterback and a center so that they can work on the center snap. The quarterback will call cadence. There will be an offensive back who he will hand the ball off to. In front of the back there will be a blocker stationed on one side of the line of scrimmage and a defensive man on the other side of the line. Everything has to be done within the three yards that you have to work with. The quarterback will call the cadence and hand off to the ball-carrier. The defensive man will try to beat the charge of the offensive man and then make the tackle.

This is the way that we indoctrinate our players into the first stages of contact. It's done gradually. We believe that the first contact that you have when you go out on the practice field is the body hitting the ground. And this is accomplished through calisthenics. The next contact we have is the body hitting the blocking sleds. These are controlled types of hits that condition the body for the violent contact that happens in the third type of contact, with one body hitting another one. This is head-on collision, full force blocking against the defensive charge. But you just don't go out there and put on a scrimmage without first taking it step by step to give the players confidence to execute all the details of their assignment.

After the Oklahoma we participate in a key drill called a five-on-five situation, which is a much tougher drill. The center, the two guards, and the two tackles go against the two defensive tackles, the two defensive ends, and the middle linebacker. Here, again, the quarterback hands off to a ball-carrier. The defensive men have to read more than one offensive blocker. The Oklahoma Drill should be won by the defensive man because all he has to do is defeat one blocker, locate the ball-carrier, and make the tackle. But in the key drill, you have to determine whether the blocker is going to come out and block you straight ahead or whether he is merely going to influence and the blocker from the outside is going to hit you. It is a much tougher drill on the defensive players. Yet, it is just another stage in developing our team to full-scale scrimmages. I like to do everything in stages. I think that to get it done properly in the scrimmages, you have to take it one step at a time.

The receivers first walk through their patterns, then jog through, and finally run full speed through the pass pattern with the quarterback throwing to them. Then we'll put on a defensive man, a linebacker, and a defensive back and have the coverages. Then we'll finally bring them together as a group and test them to see if they can take individual skills and turn them into team skills.

Another drill that I introduced to the squad is a tough one called the "gassers." We had these at the end of the morning sessions. It's running for the sake of getting your body in the best possible condition. It is vitally important during the fourth quarter of a game, or on a hot day, to have your legs strong and your wind. It helps you to be in better condition than the players you are playing against. Gassers are sprints across the field. You start out with your foot on one sideline, run over to the other sideline and touch it, come back to where you started, go back to the other sideline and return to where you started. We like to see our players run the drill from thirty to forty-five seconds—a big defensive lineman is naturally going to run slower than a fast defensive back or an outside receiver. We start out with one set of four runs. Then we start the second set of four and try to get them to do it in the same time or a better one than they did before. Then we'll break for thirty seconds and start the third set of gassers and try to finish these faster than we did the first set.

If you do the gassers conscientiously, with an eye on the watch, then a lot can be gained from them. We did them at Baltimore, but we had trouble trying to get some of the players to run them the way they should be run. However, when I first came to Miami, I was determined that I would initiate them the proper way. I explained to the players that I didn't want any shortcuts, to make sure they touched the line where they were supposed to and be certain that they ran within the proper time limits. We also wanted them to make sure that the rest period between the gassers was kept at about thirty seconds so that they would actually be forcing themselves to run. The only way they could derive any real value from this exercise was to continue to improve their times and to cut down on the time in between the gassers so that as the season progressed, they would get stronger. Once the regular season began, I would have them run the gassers only twice a week. They have been instrumental in our conditioning and there were many games that we have won because we were in better shape than our opponents. The gassers are one of the reasons.

The other drill that I initiated with the Dolphins was the twelve-minute run. This originated from Ken Cooper's Aerobics book. The objective is to see how far a person can run in twelve minutes around a measured distance. You can run this drill anywhere, a track, a football field, anywhere as long as you know the distance. I first introduced this drill during the indoctrination sessions we had before training camp. I warned the players that they would be tested again when they reported to camp. The twelve-minute run provided an incentive to keep them running and to report in the best condition possible.

When the players first reported, I'll never forget

Dick Anderson. He ran further than anybody, with the exception of one rookie who was more of a track man than a football player. Dick, who is very conscientious, worked hard to improve. When he was tested in the twelve-minute run, he ran eight laps around a quarter-mile track, which adds up to two miles. It was further than any player I've ever coached had gone. The players hated this drill, feeling that it didn't have anything to do with being a good football player. I know it helped discipline them and made them conscientious in their conditioning programs. They've been asked to do it every year and, what's more, they'll be required to do it as long as I am the head coach here, to see whether or not they have worked out before reporting to camp. It's a test of a person's endurance more than anything else and also the make-up of an individual. You find out how much pride your players have, whether or not they want to take the easy way out or really attack it and get as much distance as they possibly can in the twelve minutes.

As a football coach I want to treat everybody the same and not worry whether a player is black or white, or whether he's Catholic, Jewish, Protestant, or whatever. The only thing I want to do is to be able to judge them objectively. I feel that unless I treat everybody the same, and this is in regard to rooms or seats on an airplane or whatever, I wouldn't be actually practicing what I preach. So, the first year together I decided to mix the blacks and the whites on our rooming list and it worked out well. For example, Bob Griese and Paul Warfield roomed together; Marv Fleming and John

Stofa; Otto Stowe and Jim Del Gaizo; Curtis Johnson and Tim Foley. A simple thing like rooming assignments helped create a feeling that everybody would be treated alike and that they were going to be judged objectively. It really helped as far as the players accepting one another on their merits as opposed to worrying about where they went to school, whether they were black or white, Christian or atheist.

After about a month, I began to taper off the practice sessions. There was no way the players could stand the amount of physical strain they were being subjected to. Besides, they had started to believe in what I was trying to do. I told them it would be up to me to try and instill in them the things that I believe are necessary to win, and that's mainly to be willing to give up a lot of things that they would otherwise enjoy doing. They would have to sacrifice in order to have the feeling of total involvement. It wasn't that we were asking them to spend hours and hours under a hot sun. I just wanted them to make the time they spent on the field productive, dedicated to achieving the maximum out of their energies. I was reaching them. Csonka who had weighed 255 came to camp at 235. Little who had weighed 285–290 reported at 265. These weight reductions helped immensely in their developing into established stars.

We won our first four preseason games. It made the players believe in themselves.

After the victories, you can look back at all the hard work and laugh. Although we lost our final two exhibition games, we were convinced that we could be a good team, a winning one. It was amazing how intelligent Griese was, how quickly he picked up our system. Fleming's blocking ability enabled us to run the ball better. A trimmed-down Csonka and Little made it obvious how much their contribution was going to be to this team. And it all happened early, before training camp actually started, when these players went out on their own and worked out. They accomplished a great amount of work by their intensity in a time-shortened training camp.

I had high hopes for a winning season. Our opening game was against the Patriots in Boston. They didn't figure to be a strong team. However, we suffered our first disappointment. We were ahead 14–3, but the Patriots rallied to win 27–14. The club was primed, ready to go. We were free from any injury. But instead of winning, we got the hell kicked out of us by a team that wasn't supposed to be so good. My anger erupted after the game. I gave the squad a tongue-lashing. I told them that we were going to have to take the criticism of the media because we certainly played like we deserved it. I wanted them to walk around with their heads up but they would have to swallow their pride and accept the criticism.

However, we did win the next week. We defeated the Oilers 20–10 in Houston. The squad was determined to snap back from the opening loss. They played tough defense, displayed good offense, and didn't make a lot of errors. We won our first game as a new unit, coach and player, player and coach. It really made me feel good.

In the weeks ahead, I felt even better. After an opening loss, we had won four consecutive times. Two of those wins were against teams the Dolphins had never beaten before—Oakland and the New York Jets. We beat the Raiders 20–13 on a rainy night in the Orange Bowl. The winning touchdown was a Griese-to-Warfield pass. It was a thing of beauty, something the Miami fans had never seen before. As Warfield caught the pass, he spun away from two or three defenders and did a complete pirouette, gliding down the sideline for the winning touchdown. It was a sign of things to come, the deadly effective Griese-to-Warfield combination.

Griese and Warfield again made their presence felt the following week in New York. They were instrumental in the 20–6 triumph, the first time the Dolphins had ever won in New York. After we beat the Bills in Buffalo, 33–14, we were as good as any team in the league. We had a 4–1 record and nobody else had a better one. You could see the look of satisfaction on the faces of the players. They felt they were accomplishing something. It was a feeling they never had before in Miami. It made all the hard work of the months before seem so worthwhile.

By now fan enthusiasm was beginning to stir. It had started to build during our pre-season game against the San Francisco 49ers. In the course of the game, the defense had put up a tremendous goal line stand that turned back the 49ers, 17–7. The large crowd had given the defensive team a great ovation for their efforts. It was the first time a Miami defensive team had received such a tribute. It made tears come to my eyes because it demonstrated to me for the first time that the fans were going to be behind our football team.

They turned out in large numbers after the Buffalo win. We returned to the Orange Bowl to play the Cleveland Browns and over 75,000 fans packed the stadium. It was the largest crowd that the Dolphins had ever played before. And, wouldn't you know it, with a 4–1 record and a four-game winning streak, we played probably the worst game imaginable. We couldn't do anything right and were shut out 28–0. We blew a great opportunity to capture our fans for good. I'm sure they went away saying that this Dolphins team didn't look any better than the Dolphins teams of the past. They had been through four losing seasons and I couldn't blame them. We absolutely stunk.

I didn't know exactly what to expect the following week. We were scheduled to play the Colts in Baltimore. Baltimore fans have been known to be hostile. Now, for the first time, I was on the field as a rival coach. Thankfully, the fans were nice to me. That was the only satisfaction I derived because the Colts really stuck it to us, 35–0. I was glad to get out of Baltimore that day.

Suddenly, after such a fine start, we were now 4–3. But what was alarming was the fact that we had been blanked two games in a row. Surely we could get some relief against the Eagles in Philadelphia. We lost again, for the third straight time, 24–17. It only became close in the final quarter when we managed to score all our points after the Eagles had built a 24–0 lead. I took out

Griese in the fourth quarter and put in Stofa who managed to get us the seventeen points.

We were now 4–4 and not looking good. Before scoring against the Eagles in the final period, we had gone through eleven quarters without putting any points on the board. What had been a promising beginning was now developing into a nightmare. At times like these coaches are pressed for important decisions. There were grumblings that I should bench Griese and go to Stofa. But I still had confidence in Griese's tremendous ability. I talked privately with Stofa on the plane back to Miami. I told him that I was going to continue with Bob. I pointed out that if he was the starting quarterback and things hadn't gone well for him, I'd treat him the same way and hoped that he understood. He felt it was the thing to do because I had so much confidence in Bob. It was a pivotal decision for me, my first major one concerning a player. If I had buckled and benched Griese, it might have destroyed his confidence. He might never have responded if I needed him again. I also knew how dedicated a person he was. By keeping him as the starter, I hoped to show him that I still had faith in his ability. All the things that happened during the losing streak weren't Griese's fault. It's true he didn't play as well as he is capable of playing. However, there were some dropped passes, key penalties and we made some bad decisions.

We weren't really ready yet to execute such important maneuvers as the intricate two-minute drill before the half and at the end of the game. This was an error on my part. We tried to do too much. We actually ended up losing a lot of points in that two-minute span and it hurt us in all three losses. Trying to get too much done backfired against veteran teams. They simply took advantage of our mistakes.

My faith in Griese was rewarded the very next week against New Orleans. He put it all together and led us to a 21–10 victory. It was a big win. It snapped our losing streak and at the same time relieved Griese of a lot of pressure. When we defeated the Colts 34–17 the following week, I knew that we had begun to turn things around.

What really did it was a 20–6 victory over the Atlanta Falcons in a Monday night game that was televised nationally. The victory established our identity as a tough, hard-nosed football team. All week long we had talked about how tough and physical the Falcons were. But, we were the ones who were physical that night. We knocked the Falcons off the ball—our defense upended the Falcon blockers, swarming, gangtackling—the kind of defense you like to see. We became a physical team that had the personnel who could run with the ball and a quarterback who had the intelligence of knowing how important a running game is, directing it, mixing his passes well, and coming up with the big play. This game was one of the early milestones in the development of the Miami Dolphins as a successful team.

We rolled after that victory. We defeated the Patriots 37–20, the Jets 16–10, and the Bills 45–7. We finished with a record of 10-4 and qualified for the playoffs. What a feeling of accomplishment! The players felt they were capable of playing anybody and challenging for the world championship. After four frustrating years, the Dolphins were winners. We not only had a winning record, but were also championship contenders. Who would ever have said that we could get so much done in so short a time as one season?

Our first-round game as the wild-card team in the playoffs was against the Oakland Raiders. We left Miami on Christmas Day for Oakland. When we arrived there, we learned it had been raining all week. The Raiders played the 49ers on a muddy field in the final game of the year and although the field was covered after the game, it never did dry out. On Christmas night, Robbie took the entire squad to San Francisco to celebrate Christmas. He made it as nice as he could for our players, realizing that they were away from their families on such an important day. It was the nicest thing that could have happened and it was something that Robbie didn't have to do. But again it just demonstrated how interested he was in getting our team ready to play and making them feel as much at home as they could.

The Raiders were a veteran team that had been involved in championship games before. The odds were against us. Although Oakland scored first, we battled back on a Griese-to-Warfield pass that tied the score 7–7 at half time. However, the Raiders made two big plays in the second half that won the game. The first was by defensive back Willie Brown in the third period. He intercepted a Griese pass and went fifty yards for a touchdown. Then in the fourth period, when we were fighting to get back into the game, we tried a safety blitz. Oakland's quarterback Daryle Lamonica read it; he threw a bomb to Rod Sherman that covered eighty-two yards and gave them a 21–7 lead. We scored near the end of the game on a pass from Griese to Willie Richardson, but it was too late. The game was lost and our season had suddenly ended.

Despite the loss, I liked the attitude of the players in the quiet dressing room after the game. They weren't satisfied at being in the playoffs, they wanted to win. I thanked them for their efforts this first season. We had come a long way and I, too, was disappointed that we didn't win. Someday, we could reach back and gain from the experience of having played in this playoff game.

Nobody said anything. The players just sat there shaking their heads. I knew that they would be back. They didn't like the taste of defeat.

10

The gloom that showed on Larry Csonka's face following the loss to Oakland was still fresh in my mind. He
sat in the locker room dejectedly, staring straight
ahead as if his football career was over. It was a look of
utter disappointment. His face mirrored the entire feeling of the squad. The players were damn unhappy
about what happened to them in Oakland. There
wasn't any comfort knowing that we finished with a
10–4 record. Instead of feeling they had accomplished
enough by getting into the playoffs, they were extremely unhappy about losing to Oakland, a team we
had beaten in the regular season. Yet, it was another
good example of getting something out of defeat, something positive surfacing from adversity. The entire
squad made up its mind after the defeat that they were
going to be better the next year. It was a quiet vow.

However, something was wrong. Very seriously
wrong. Early in the year Kiick and Csonka were in a

salary dispute with management. Players are constantly involved with management regarding salaries on every club around the league. But this was something else again. Both had said that if they weren't signed by the time that training camp opened, they wouldn't report. It was the first double holdout in professional football history and I didn't like it. For the second straight year my training camp schedule had been interrupted. The previous year it was the players' strike. This time it was Csonka and Kiick upsetting my work schedule. How could we even think about improving our record with my two starting runners nowhere in sight?

Larry and Jim were represented by the same agent, Ed Keating who works for the Mark McCormack Agency in Cleveland. McCormack had represented Paul Warfield the year before when we acquired him from the Browns. Through Warfield, he got to know Csonka and Kiick. Keating, realizing that he represented both our backs, decided that the best way to negotiate their salaries was to do it together. They were both seeking the same salary. In management's view, they were two separate players and the Dolphins refused to negotiate their contracts together. Joe Thomas, who was doing the negotiating for the Dolphins, had some heated meetings with Keating. Both sides refused to budge, Thomas on dealing with each player separately and Keating from his position of bargaining for both collectively.

I don't make it a practice to get involved with player contracts. I leave those matters to the front office. All I was concerned with at the moment was preparing the Dolphins for the 1971 season and hopefully a trip to the Super Bowl. The Kiick and Csonka situation didn't help matters. I had heard strong reports that they wouldn't be in camp. Yet, knowing the desire these two players had, I felt that they would report with the rest of the squad. When training camp opened Kiick and Csonka were absent.

I had told the squad our first year together that I would treat each one of them equally. Kiick and Csonka were no exceptions. I announced to the squad that according to the scale of fines listed in our book, Kiick and Csonka would be fined for every day they were out of camp. Rules are made for everyone. They must be adhered to or a serious disciplinary problem can develop. Discipline is a word that is foremost in my book. And after strongly emphasizing it, we went ahead with our regular training camp program without Kiick and Csonka.

While concentrating on the work to be done, I also had to keep abreast of what was happening with the Kiick and Csonka salary squabble. I most certainly didn't want the situation to disrupt the squad. But it could get stickier with each passing day. Every effort was being made to get the players to agree to terms. Unfortunately, Thomas was hospitalized. He had a heart by-pass operation the year before and now he had developed hepatitis. While the negotiations reached a stalemate, Robbie was in Europe. The situation was getting serious.

Finally, Robbie returned and picked up where

Thomas left off. A couple of days after he was back, the two players agreed to sign their contracts separately. The signing actually took place in Thomas's hospital room. I know the coaching staff and the players were relieved when Jim and Larry finally signed and reported to camp. They had missed a lot of work and they would also be missing $2,000 each from their paychecks. One thing was made definite, they would have to pay the fines. There wasn't any thought of rescinding them.

We didn't make many personnel changes on the squad. George Mira came aboard in the off-season as a free agent to compete against Stofa for the backup spot behind Griese. Stofa got hurt and Mira snapped back from a sore arm to win the reserve role. The year before we had managed to get Paul Warfield from Cleveland for a first-round draft choice. This time we acquired Bob Matheson, a linebacker, from the Browns for a No. 2 draft pick. Matheson gave us good backup at that position and was capable of playing the middle or the outside. We had one rookie, Otto Stowe, a wide receiver with good speed, who we were anxious to see. We didn't have a No. 1 draft choice, since that was awarded to the Baltimore Colts. Stowe was actually our first-draft choice and we selected him as the first player on the second round. The overall squad was still the same and we maintained the same basic offensive and defensive alignments.

Kiick and Csonka arrived in camp a week before our first pre-season game. They both knew what was expected of them. Still, they had work to catch up on and

I had to ask them to do it. They knew how much the squad wanted to win this year and they most certainly didn't want to be the ones to let them down. There was a feeling of a championship in the air.

I wanted to utilize our training camp to minimize last year's mistakes and felt that Bob Griese was the key. I consider him a no-fault quarterback. He has a complete understanding of all offensive situations and makes very few errors himself. This would be his second year of working with Warfield, of getting their timing synchronized.

Defensively, we needed improvement on our line. The pass rush in particular was weak. We were the worst pass rushing team in the AFC during 1970, despite our 10–4 record. This year we had to get to the passer more often. We worked on the problem during the off-season and sent out weight training programs to the linemen. We even flew some to Miami to be checked individually. I noticed the desire of our players to work on these off-season programs. It showed an important thing: attitude.

In 1970 there were so many unknowns. The first year we found out what it took to win. In 1971, our primary objective was to be a consistent winner, to gain the poise and confidence that would be necessary to eventually compete for the world championship. We also had to learn how to come from behind. I felt much better about our chances this time.

Kiick and Csonka played only briefly in our first pre-season game. It wasn't until the third or fourth game that they started to round into shape. However, our record wasn't a good one, 2–3–1. Up until the last pre-season game against Minnesota, I was satisfied with the progress we had made. But when we were blanked by the Vikings 24–0, I was really concerned.

We were favored to win our opening game of the regular season against the Denver Broncos. We didn't play a good game at all, and were fortunate to settle for a 10–10 tie. At half time, the score was 3–3. Denver went ahead 10–3 in the second half and we were having trouble moving the ball. We didn't get the tying touchdown until late in the fourth quarter when Griese hit Warfield on a slant-in that covered thirty-one yards. We had a number of chances to win but Garo Yepremian missed four field goals and then Jake Scott took a punt return to within easy field goal distance but fumbled the ball and Denver recovered.

Lou Saban, the head coach of the Broncos, decided to run the clock out and play for a tie. He made a statement after the game that half a loaf is better than none. I think it really hurt him with the fans and the Denver press.

The talk after the game in front of the squad was designed to give Garo and Scott a lot of confidence. It showed them that we weren't fickle, that we'd pat them on the back when we won and not talk about them behind their backs when we lost. The entire squad felt the way I did and this vote of confidence was very helpful in the emergence of Yepremian as a consistent kicker. This was evident the very next week when Yepremian booted five field goals in our 29–14 victory over the Bills in Buffalo. I thought everything would be all right after that win but I was mistaken. The following week we lost to the New York Jets 14–10 in the Orange Bowl. The game had a weird ending. We were leading the Jets 10–0 midway through the fourth period. The Jets then pushed across a touchdown but we were still ahead 10–7 and not in any immediate danger when Steve O'Neal, the Jets's punter, punted short to his right. Dick Anderson didn't see the ball as he was coming over to block and the ball hit the ground, bounced up, and hit Anderson. The Jets pounced on it. So, instead of having the ball with only a couple of minutes left to play and great field position, the Jets recovered.

We had blown a 10–0 lead and lost to a team that we had completely dominated. It was a bitter pill to swallow. The Jets beat us with second-string quarterback Al Woodall, who took over for Namath because of a broken leg Joe suffered in a pre-season game. So far, we had blown a game that we should have won and tied a game that we also should have won. It was a bad beginning. Instead of being 3–0, we were 1–1–1. And, we were lucky to be that because the Denver game could have gone either way.

We were at a pretty low ebb as we prepared to play Cincinnati in the fourth game of the season in Cincinnati. The Bengals were better than any of the three teams we had played. A loss could knock us out of contention because Baltimore was off to a fast start in our division. The night before the game I asked the squad to take some time after the 9:30 snack to meet on their own. I called the coaches out of their rooms and let the players meet privately, and I know that this is where some of the leadership from within took place. I think Griese made some strong comments in the meeting and so did Csonka, Buoniconti, and Warfield. Allowing them to meet this particular night enabled them to pull together a little bit more.

Well, we put it together against Cincinnati. We completely dominated in winning 23–13. This was our finest game, both offensively and defensively, and made us feel pretty good about the prospects for the rest of the season. We were now 2–1–1 and Baltimore, who had lost, was 3–1. So, we weren't far away from first place, but we had to keep it going.

The victory over the Bengals was the beginning of an eight-game winning streak that was the longest in the league that year. In beating New England 41–3 the following week, Griese threw three touchdown passes on three consecutive plays. Bim, bim, bim. Just like that. It was the first time I had ever seen this happen. Griese started to demonstrate that he had killer instinct and the ability to confuse the defense. After his first touchdown pass, we got the ball back on an interception. On first down, Griese threw a touchdown pass. The Patriots fumbled the kickoff and we recovered. Instead of working the ball in, Griese stepped back and fired his third touchdown pass. It was a great performance and a sign of things to come in a year in which he was voted the outstanding player in the American Football Conference.

We were beginning to put it all together now. We faced the Jets in New York and revenged our earlier defeat, 30–14. Despite the muddy ground, both Kiick and Csonka were fantastic. They gained over a hundred yards each. It didn't look as if we were ready to play after the Jets first series. They took the ball and moved all the way for a touchdown. But the key play that turned it around for us was Griese's thirty-seven-yard touchdown pass to Warfield just before the half. It put us on top, 10–7, and we went on from there.

I was especially gratified with our 20–14 triumph over the Los Angeles Rams the next week. They treated us as if we were from a minor league. The Los Angeles people were NFL oriented and knew very little about the Dolphins. They knew a little bit about me in the years that I competed against the Rams while I was at Baltimore. They knew a little bit about Warfield and Fleming. We could have been from Disneyland for that matter. We broke on top, 17–0, and then managed to hang in on the way to a 17–14 victory as the Rams scored both their touchdowns in the final quarter. It was a very meaningful game in that we managed to beat one of the old powers of the NFL in their home stadium. Our defense was really hitting. I can't say enough about them. They hung in there and made the big play time and time again.

Another milestone in our development occurred the next week. This was a victory over Pittsburgh in Miami, 24–21. It was extremely important because in this game our team learned to come from behind. Griese spent the entire night before the game in a hospital with a stomach disorder. He was fed intravenously and was released from the hospital the morning

of the game. When he reported to the Orange Bowl I
had to look twice. Bob looked pale and fatigued, and I
didn't think he would be able to play. I told him I
would start Mira and use him only if I thought it was
absolutely necessary. However, we fell behind early in
the second quarter, 21–3. I could see that Mira couldn't
get the job done. I looked over at Bob on the bench.
He knew I was thinking about putting him in. I didn't
have to ask him. He got up, walked over toward me,
and said, "I'm ready." On his first play, Griese fumbled
the snap and the Steelers recovered. But our defense
held and we got the ball back again. Griese moved
quickly. He got us two touchdowns before the half,
which put us back into the game, trailing only 21–17.
Then in the fourth period he hit Warfield with the
winning touchdown pass that covered sixty yards for a
24–21 victory. It was in this game that the squad really
developed the confidence that proved we were capable
of coming from behind. It was an important stepping
stone as far as I was concerned.

The next game was a crucial one. It was against the
Colts in Miami. We were 7–1–1 and they were 7–2. Baltimore had a 7–0 lead in the third period. But Kiick
scored from a yard out and then minutes later Griese
hit Fleming with a touchdown pass to put us ahead.
The Colts succeeded in tying the game at 14–14 before
Yepremian won it with a twenty-yard field goal in the
final period, 17–14. It was a big win for us because we
had defeated the defending world champions. The
players, knowing how I felt about beating my old
team, gave me the game ball. However, I gave it to

Csonka. He played on a bad leg and played one of the gutsiest games I ever saw. Despite his injury, he gained ninety-three yards on fifteen carries.

We convinced a lot of people across the country in our next appearance. It was a Monday night game on national television against the Chicago Bears in the Orange Bowl. We completely dominated play and won convincingly, 34–3 in a near-perfect game. We played exceptionally well both ways, offensively and defensively. Even the speciality teams did an excellent job. Csonka again had a great game, gaining over a hundred yards. He is a throwback to the old-time fullback, like Bronco Nagurski, the classic brute-power-type runner. For a time we seemed to be getting back to the 210-pound players at fullback. But where else do you find a combination of Csonka's abilities in a 235-pound package?

Ahead of us were the Patriots whom we had easily beaten earlier, 41–3. It was a cold day in New England and we were even colder. They upset us 34–13. They dominated after Mercury Morris returned the opening kickoff ninety-four yards. Quarterback Jim Plunkett and his prime receiver Randy Vataha tore us apart. Their defense did a tremendous job on double covering our outside receivers. They forced us to go to the tight end and we weren't successful. They outcoached us, outhit us, and did everything in a game they could think of in winning. All week long I had been trying to guard against a letdown of any type after the easy victory over the Bears. But until you're out on the field, you just don't really know what's going to happen to your team. We weren't emotionally involved in the game and they simply beat us—and that was partly my fault.

Our lead over the Colts now was only a half game and I knew they would be waiting for us in Baltimore. Unitas skillfully executed two long ball control drives against us in the first half. Both of them consumed about ten minutes on the clock and he made the maximum use of both drives to score two touchdowns. They were ahead 14–0 at the half and all we could do was to score a field goal in the second half against their great defense. They won 14–3 and we lost our second game in a row, falling a half game behind the Colts with only one more game remaining on the regular season schedule.

Our final game was against the Green Bay Packers, while the Colts were playing the Patriots at home. We were aware that a victory over the Packers and a loss by the Colts would not only give us the Eastern Division title but would also have a bearing where the AFC championship game would be played. So, we went after Green Bay real hard, played a good game against a fine team, and won 27–6. It was an important win because New England upset Baltimore 21–17. Miami had its first divisional championship. After two lackluster performances, the squad snapped back. We had figured all along that we would be playing Cleveland, since the Colts were expected to beat the Patriots. So, we scouted Cleveland and then suddenly we were scheduled to play Kansas City instead.

The opening playoff game between Miami and Kansas City was one of the most important games ever played. It was a real classic. It has always been written that the Colts-Giants sudden-death overtime championship game of 1958 was the greatest game ever played. I disagree. I think the greatest game was the one that was played on Christmas Day 1971. It was the longest game in the history of professional football, eighty-two minutes and forty seconds. That's a lot of football, a lot of tension, and a lot of thrills. We beat the Chiefs in Kansas City 27–24 and earned a berth in the AFC championship game. For us, it was another milestone in the development of a world championship team. The year before we had to learn how to win. In 1971 we had to learn any number of factors that go hand in hand with winning—poise, coming from behind, and having players come off the bench to contribute when someone was injured. The squad also learned what it took to be consistent—an eight-game winning streak. This kind of consistency was needed to gain the playoffs. The winning streak was extremely vital in that it occurred after a poor 1–1–1 start. All these positive things happened during the course of the season. The Dolphins were growing up.

Unexpectedly, we prepared to meet Kansas City. They presented a problem not only because we had scouted the Browns instead of the Chiefs on the final day of the season, but also because we hadn't faced any team with the variety of formations that the Chiefs used. They featured a multiple offense and a stack defense, which we weren't too familiar with.

Quickly we went to work. Defensively, we planned

to keep it as simple as possible. We didn't want to get confused against the multiple formations, the shifting, and the man in motion that are characteristic of Coach Hank Stram's team. The formations and the motion and the other things he did served to camouflage his real intent, which was to beat you physically up front and have you make errors in your secondary that would enable their receivers to get open for cheap touchdowns. By playing it simple on defense we wouldn't get suckered into making mistakes. In essence, we wanted to oversimplify what the Chiefs were doing. All we told the defense to do was to worry about what was going to happen after the ball was snapped, not before. I wanted to guard against getting into a man-on-man situation with their wide receivers. So, we emphasized coverage in the middle and making sure that the two deep zones were covered. This would prevent a receiver from getting wide open in the middle for the cheap touchdown. That's why we stressed simplicity. We had to play our own game.

Offensively, we figured we had to find some running room inside their stacked defense. They had a distinct style in their secondary. Their cornerbacks Jim Marsalis and Emmit Thomas played bump-and-run against the wide receivers. Safety Johnny Robinson was given a lot of freedom. Yet, we felt that if we got into passing situations against this style of coverage we would be able to beat them. The feeling was that Griese would be able to take advantage of the one-on-one coverages on the outside. Warfield certainly would be able to beat anybody who was playing him man-for-man.

Twilley, on the other side, would present a big challenge on a one-and-one-situation. If we could establish the running game and hit with the quick pass, then we could pretty much control the game.

We arrived in Kansas City on Christmas Eve and I learned that the league was going to announce the selection of the players for the AFC Pro Bowl. That's fine. But not at a time like this. I didn't want anything, especially something like this, to detract from our players' concentration. All Star selections could be disappointing to some players. Especially when they feel they will be named to the team. I know Yepremian felt this way after the season he had. I knew the announcement would break in the newspapers, so I decided to tell my players the results. They would have read it for themselves anyway and that could have been worse psychologically. Here they are preparing for what could be their biggest game of the season and they had to worry about something like this. I told them not to worry about an All-Star game. Here is where it's all at.

The weather was over 60 degrees on the day of the game, which was quite unusual for Kansas City at that time of the year. We received the kickoff but had trouble getting our offense moving in the first period. The running attack wasn't working. Their defense split real wide and succeeded in containing us and keeping us inside. Their middle linebacker Willie Lanier, in my estimation one of the finest in the game, was dominating play. We were also having trouble handling Curley Culp. He is a strong defensive lineman who was doing a great job standing up our center and making the plays on the inside. Our play would start out like there would be a big hole to run to, but quickly we were shut off by Culp, Lanier, and tackle Buck Buchanan. So, instead of getting the four or five yards that we were going for on first down, we were ending up with two or three.

Meanwhile, the Chiefs had no trouble moving the ball. In fact, they scored the first two times they had it. Jan Stenerud kicked a twenty-four-yard field goal, then Len Dawson hit Ed Podolak with a seven-yard touchdown pass, and before you could say Merry Christmas, we were behind 10–0. However, we didn't panic and we didn't deviate from our game plan. We started to put things together in the second quarter. Griese took us on a drive to score our first touchdown. Then, in the final minute of the first half, Yepremian booted a fourteen-yard field goal to tie the score 10–10. I felt a lot better about things at the half. We were down 10–0, but we didn't fold. Instead, we kept our poise and bounced back to tie the game. In so doing, we controlled the game in the second period after Kansas City had clearly dominated play in the first quarter.

The Chiefs executed great ball control in scoring a touchdown in the third period to go ahead 17–10. They used up over nine minutes on the clock. We didn't have much time left when we got the ball. Yet, Griese called an excellent series of plays and got us the tying touchdown with only about a minute remaining. So, when the third period ended the score was tied at 17–17. My hope now was to stop the Chiefs and get in front ourselves. We were in the position of playing catch-up throughout the entire game.

However, we were victimized by the big play that I warned the defense about. Dawson connected with his wide receiver Elmo Wright for a sixty-three-yard play that gave them excellent position on our three-yard line. They moved in for the touchdown, which once again put them in front, 24–17. Time was running out. There were only about six minutes left in the game when Griese took over the offense. He demonstrated the poise so necessary to bring a team back. Twice he connected on passes in critical third-down situations. And, with a little over a minute to play, he fired a touchdown pass to Fleming for a 24–24 tie. In the face of mounting pressure, Griese had connected on five straight passes during the drive. It really gave us a boost, coming from behind with a long drive under pressure to tie the game.

My heart almost stopped beating on the kickoff. Ed Podolak, who had a big game, took the kickoff on the goal line and started up field. He found some running room and broke into the open past midfield. It looked as if he was going to go all the way. But Yepremian moved toward him. Podolak saw him and lost a step changing direction in an effort to avoid Yepremian. The slight delay enabled Curtis Johnson to angle over and knock Podolak out of bounds on the twenty-two-yard line. Johnson had saved a touchdown, but what excellent field position the Chiefs had. They were in certain field goal distance. Podolak ran straight ahead three consecutive times. The defense stopped him from advancing the ball further. On fourth down, Stenerud came in to attempt a thirty-one-yard field goal. It was a chip shot. I could only pray that he'd miss. There were only thirty-one seconds left. The entire outcome of the game rested on Stenerud's kick. We put a little pressure on him. Lloyd Mumphord came in tough as Stenerud got his kick off. It looked like he hurried it a little. The kick missed. I couldn't believe it. The missed field goal gave us new life. I could feel it on the sidelines. The players were all full of energy despite having played a tough, physical game.

The game was sent into sudden death. And, for a young team that hadn't been exposed to a pressure situation like this, the odds certainly favored Kansas City, a veteran team that had been involved in championship games before. To make matters worse, we lost the flip of the coin and had to kick off. Kansas City would get the first opportunity to score. If they did, it would be all over. We had to hold them. Yepremian kicked the ball deep, out of the end zone. However, one of our players in his eagerness to get downfield to cover the kick, was offsides. The Chiefs got a break. Instead of putting the ball in play on their twenty, they would get another chance to run it back. Yepremian's kick was short and Podolak ran it back to the Chiefs's forty-six-yard line. Kansas City had great field position. They worked the ball to our thirty-five and again Stenerud came in to try a field goal. Could he miss again? Although the distance was longer than the other one, Stenerud is an accurate long-distance kicker. I held my breath as the ball was snapped. Buoniconti broke through, leaped, and blocked the kick. Now we had a chance on offense. However, the closest we could get was to the Chiefs's forty-five-yard line. Yepremian tried a fifty-two-yard field goal but it was no good. Still, when the first overtime period ended, we had possession of the ball.

After five periods, we had managed to play even. But, our defense was getting much stronger and our offense was showing a lot more movement. In a game like this, certainly condition plays a big part. With our emphasis on conditioning all through training camp, the gassers, the twelve-minute run, I knew that we wouldn't get beat because we weren't in shape to play. We had the ball on our own thirty-yard line and Griese had us moving. After Kiick gained five yards, Griese reached back into our game plan and called a play that we hadn't used the entire game. He felt he was in a situation where he had to come up with something and called Csonka's number on a "roll right, trap left." The play would start out to the right with guard Larry Little and tackle Norm Evans leading the way. Then Csonka would quickly change direction and cut to his left. The play worked perfectly. Kansas City in its eagerness to get to the ball left the middle wide open. Csonka burst through for twenty-nine yards. He finally was stopped by Jim Kearney, the Chiefs's safety, on the Kansas City thirty-six-yard line. I looked up and suddenly we were in great field position. I was thinking field goal at this point. We used the next three downs to set it up. On fourth down, we were on the thirty-yard line and I sent in Yepremian to kick the most important field goal of his life from thirty-seven yards out. I bent over with my hands on my knees to watch. The snap was good, the hold by Karl Noonan was good, and Yepremian's kick was good. Unbelievable! Coming back time after time in a highly pressurized game, we won the longest game ever played, 27–24. I was the happiest guy alive. It was the most important win I ever enjoyed. There had been a lot of disappointments. But this victory in double overtime by a young team against a veteran one, showing the class, the poise to get the job done, was tremendous.

It was a Christmas I'll never forget. The happiness, the excitement in the dressing room, the magnitude of what happened on the field, really didn't hit me until I was on the plane returning to Miami. Quietly in my mind, I replayed the game. I thought about it: the defense; the offense; the pressure; the suspense; the excitement; and finally Yepremian's kick soaring in the night right through the middle of the crossbars. How many coaches can experience a moment like this? I was burning with pride at what my team had accomplished. They never quit. I can't minimize the pressure they were subjected to. Yet they hung tough and fought back and won the biggest victory of their lives in such a dramatic ending. Every day should be Christmas.

The excitement was not over. Not by a long shot. Even though it was Christmas night, a night most people like to spend at home, the airport was ringed with people. Our fans were so excited about the win that they wanted to share the happiness with us. I couldn't believe my eyes at the sight of the mob. There were an estimated 15,000 to 25,000 people at the airport. I have never witnessed anything like that in my life. It was going to be practically impossible to get through the crowd. It was wall-to-wall people. They were stacked up on top of each other, standing, straining, cheering, all wanting to be part of the excitement, the happiness, all Miami Dolphins's fans.

Somehow, we finally managed to get through the mass of humanity to the parking lot, to our cars, and finally to start on the way home. I had my son David with me and luckily we didn't get separated by the crowd. I got behind the wheel, closed the door, and released a sigh of relief. I turned the key in the ignition but nothing happened. I tried again, still nothing. I kept pumping my foot on the accelerator. Still the motor didn't start. I kept trying. It was futile. After a few minutes I gave up. It was obvious that the battery was dead. David looked at me.

"What now, dad?"

"Well, it's apparent we'll never make it home in this car."

"Got any suggestions?"

"At this moment the only thing I can think about is hitching a ride home."

"You're kidding, dad."

"No, I'm not. Do you have a better idea?"

"No."

"Okay, let's get going."

So, we got our luggage together, locked the car, left

it in the parking lot, and walked toward the main entrance of the airport. There were hundreds of cars around. David and I stuck out our thumbs. The first car that approached stopped. The woman who was sitting on the passenger side in the front seat recognized me. I asked her if she was going toward Miami Lakes. She said no, but that she would take me anyplace I wanted to go. So, David and I got into the car. There was another couple in the back seat and we all headed to my home with the horns of over a hundred cars blaring away. I invited them into the house for a Christmas drink. Naturally we began talking football and replayed the game against the Kansas City Chiefs over and over. It was a day and a night I'll always remember. I had to be the first coach in history to win a playoff game and end up hitching a ride home.

I couldn't savor the victory too long. The next day the Colts beat the Browns, which meant that we had to play Baltimore for the AFC championship in a week. I was thankful for one thing, the game would be played in the Orange Bowl. We had lost both times we played in Baltimore and had failed to score a touchdown in either game. That's why beating Green Bay on the final day of the season was so important. It gave us a 10–3–1 record while Baltimore finished 10–4. Had the Colts finished ahead of us, the AFC championship game would have been played in Baltimore. I felt we had an advantage playing in the Orange Bowl, since it was our home field and we had twice beaten Baltimore there quite easily.

The game had an extra incentive for me personally. I

now was presented with the opportunity of knocking the Colts out of the competition for the world championship. I relished the thought. In just two years since I left Baltimore, I was facing my old team in a championship game. How sweet a victory would be.

After the dramatic triumph over Kansas City, I was confident. So were the players. They realized what they had accomplished against the Chiefs. They were determined not to stop winning now. What we had to guard against was allowing Unitas to control the ball the way he did against us three weeks before. The linebackers were instructed not to react immediately on pass plays. The idea was to get Unitas to commit himself first before reacting. In that way, the linebackers could pick up the backs coming out of the backfield with the short pass. I felt this slight adjustment would be enough to hamper Unitas. If we could stop him, then break on top, we could pretty much control the action.

Near the end of the first period, Griese called a play-action pass. The execution was perfect and it caught the Colts off balance. Rex Kern, a rookie cornerback, overreacted when Griese faked a hand-off to Csonka. When Griese straightened up to pass, he found Warfield all alone streaking down the sideline in the area Kern had vacated. The pass was perfectly timed and Warfield streaked all alone for a touchdown that covered seventy-five yards. It was a startling play that burned the Colts and gave us momentum. Our defense picked it up. On a key fourth down and one play on our nine-yard line near the end of the half, the

Colts decided to gamble. Instead of going for a field goal that would have made the score 7–3, they sought a first down. In a great effort, led by Buoniconti, the defense stopped fullback Don Nottingham on a dive play in midair.

Toward the end of the third period, the defense again came up with another dramatic play. Only more so. On third down, Unitas dropped back to pass. He tried to hit his wide receiver Eddie Hinton. However, Curtis Johnson covered the play well and deflected the ball. Dick Anderson caught it and began a broken field run to the goal line that was sixty-two yards away. It was a picture play, one that couldn't be taught. As Anderson started to run, he picked up blocks one after the other. In all, he received six of the most beautifully timed blocks that I have ever seen in all the years I have been in football. They weren't just delay blocks. The blocks were executed so perfectly that they wiped out the Colt players in precision fashion all over the field. The final block was delivered by Bob Heinz on Unitas, and Anderson cut behind to score. The 78,629 fans in the Orange Bowl exploded. So did our squad on the sideline. We went ahead 14–0 and felt that victory was ours.

Griese clinched it in the fourth period. He made another excellent call that burned the Colts. On a third down and two from our forty-five, he noticed that the Colts were in a man-on-man coverage. He decided on a pass to Warfield and worked it perfectly. Warfield got behind the Colts's secondary and Griese hit him with a pass that carried for fifty yards to the five.

When Csonka went over on the next play, we knew it was all over. The only thing the defense wanted was a shutout. The Colts hadn't been shut out in ninety-six games. That's what the defense was aiming for and they got it. A 21–0 shutout that gave Miami its first AFC championship.

We finished the season with the best rushing attack in the NFL with 2,429 yards. Our team rushing average was also the best, five yards a run. Larry Csonka topped the runners in the NFL with a 5.4 yard average per carry. Bob Griese was the passing leader and was later voted the outstanding player in the AFC. Paul Warfield averaged twenty-three yards a catch and led the league with eleven touchdown passes. Garo Yepremian was the scoring leader of the NFL with 117 points. He had the most field goals, 28, and the best field goal percentage, 70 percent. Individual honors are fine, but when they contribute to a team championship, so much the better. We had won the AFC title just two years after the Dolphins were the laughingstock of the league. Now everyone realized that the 1970 season wasn't a fluke. The Dolphins weren't pushovers anymore.

I was too excited to start planning about the Super Bowl. I wanted to savor the astonishing victory over the Colts. At midnight the same night, the game was presented on television. I was too happy to think about sleeping. I told Dorothy that she would have to spare me a few more hours of this long day. Her mother and father were visiting us so they all decided to watch the game with me. At about 1:30 in the morning the telephone rang. "Who could it be?" I wondered out loud. I figured it was a reporter. When I picked up the phone and answered it, I gulped. A voice on the other end told me that the White House was calling and that the president would like to talk to me. I put my hand over the receiver and said to my in-laws that the president is calling. They couldn't believe it and neither could I really. I thought somebody was pulling my leg. What would the president be doing calling me at 1:30 in the morning? I hung on and a moment later someone spoke. I recognized the voice as President Nixon's.

"Coach Shula, I want to personally congratulate you on the great effort that your team displayed today in winning the championship."

"Thank you very much, Mr. President."

Then he started to talk technical football. I was very surprised by his knowledge.

"The Cowboys are a fine football team and Coach Landry is an exceptional coach."

"You're right, sir."

"Coach, I think it would be a good idea for you to use a pass that you throw to Warfield."

"What pass, sir?"

"You know, that slant-in pattern where Warfield starts down and then breaks into the middle of the field."

"Yes, Mr. President, we do plan on using that slant-in pass to Warfield against the Cowboys."

"I think it can work for a big gain."

"Yes, sir, it can."

"Well, again my congratulations on a fine victory."

"Thank you for taking the time to call and for your interest in professional football, Mr. President."

I'm aware that the president has been chided about paying so much attention to sports and his phone calls to coaches after major games. I think it is wonderful that he takes an interest in sports because it is such a part of the American way of life. I also recalled that after the bitter Super Bowl loss to the Jets when no one was calling or writing me, President Nixon, then the president-elect, took the time to write me a letter. He said that the knew how disappointed I was in not winning the game, but he had been a loser who had just turned a winner. He felt that if I continued to work and believe in myself that I would be able to turn it around. The president didn't forget about a loser.

11

The inflammatory remarks never seem to end. I no sooner got to New Orleans when George Wilson fired a verbal fusillade. He was quoted by a newspaper in Miami as saying, "Joe Doakes could have taken this Miami team to the American Football Conference championship and the Super Bowl." When I had replaced him as coach two years ago, George felt that he should have had another season. He was very disappointed and bitter that Robbie did not give him the extra year that he believed Joe had promised him. I have always given Wilson credit for the early development of the Dolphins. I pointed that out when I took the job; that he, Robbie, and Joe Thomas were certainly responsible for bringing the Dolphins along as far as they had. I also remarked that any success I hoped to have in the future would be partially based on the foundation they built. But, let's face it, when I took over as coach, the team had won only three games. Wilson's bitter attack on my coaching ability surprised me. Although our relationship was cool after I had replaced him, we had met occasionally and always spoke to each other. I didn't realize how bitter he was inside until his statements appeared in the newspaper. It's my nature when something like this confronts me to attack it head on. At a press conference the next day, I began my remarks by saying, "Hi, I'm Don Shula not Joe Doakes."

Yet, the Wilson episode did upset me. I guess everything in life can't always be flowery. You have to be strong enough to take the attacks, to roll with the punches. One thing I knew, it wasn't going to deter me from preparing my squad to win a Super Bowl.

I had begun these preparations over a week ago in Miami. The club was still keyed up when they reported for practice on Wednesday. They were full of excitement at winning the AFC championship. We had a number of preliminary practices scheduled at Biscayne College prior to leaving for New Orleans on Sunday. Although the players appeared loose, the work on the field was so high-keyed, so intense, so productive that it left me wondering. I didn't want to think that we were too good; we have to be careful, we're working too hard. I knew that there was a long time between now and the Super Bowl. I felt that with the layoff for travel on Sunday and the picture day on Monday in New Orleans, things would come back to normal.

The sessions at Biscayne were excellent with a great deal of concentration. However, I think that during this period players who normally acted naturally were now trying to act another way. Some players who normally are serious went around trying to keep the squad loose by saying funny things. It wasn't a natural thing. I cautioned the players about it at a squad meeting. I wanted them to do the things we had done before the Kansas City game and before the AFC championship game against Baltimore. It was really their first experience at this type of thing.

I had been through a Super Bowl week before with Baltimore in 1969. It was evident that the league had learned a great deal from past Super Bowl experiences, and they did everything to accommodate us as best they could. However, we were housed at the Fontainebleau, which was in a pretty busy area, while the Cowboys stayed out near the airport. They had more security and less problems with visitors in the lobby and around the hotel. We were constantly mobbed by autograph seekers. Yet, the league did an effective job of scheduling press conferences and everything was pretty well controlled. We tried to cooperate with them, although the scene in the lobby was just ridiculous at times because of the great number of people who were staying in the hotel.

The workouts we had in New Orleans were in sharp contrast to the ones we had in Miami. Our momentum seemed to be going the wrong way. Did the squad peak in Miami? Did they leave the game on the field back there? Maybe too much emphasis was placed on the workouts in Miami. Perhaps we should have eased up then with the game still almost two weeks away.

Possibly it would have been better to point toward an emotional and physical peak in our practice sessions in New Orleans. Whatever, something didn't look right and it was hard to put my finger on it.

Recognizing that the players would have a problem finding a place to eat the night before the game, I thought it would be a good idea if we all dined together. I went one step further. I suggested that we take the players' wives, who were arriving the same evening on the team charter from Miami, with us. We would have an early, quiet dinner and then bring the players back to the hotel, skipping the 9:30 snack that we normally have and just check them in at 11:30. Dinner was arranged at a very fine restaurant on the outskirts of the city. It was an enjoyable evening. The only difference was that this wasn't what we had done during our eight-game winning streak during the season, or the night before the playoff game in Kansas City or before the AFC championship game in Miami. I think it was a mistake on my part. How important it was to the final outcome of the game, I really don't know. But if I had it to do all over again, I certainly wouldn't do it again.

There was a great deal of difference between the Dolphins and the Colt squad I had in the 1969 Super Bowl. Basically, the Colts were a veteran team that had been playing together a long time. They knew each other in and out and had performed well. In virtually every respect the Colts were a seasoned club, solid in every department. They had a tremendous defensive unit that had a great record. The Colts had won more games in one year, thirteen, than any other football team in history.

On the other hand, the Dolphins were basically a young team. They were just beginning to play to their potential. Griese and Warfield were outstanding with the aerial game and Csonka and Kiick were devastating with the ground attack. What stands out in my mind is that Larry and Jim went through an entire year and the playoffs with only one fumble between them. Kiick had fumbled against New England. Their achievement was remarkable. It was our trademark, a team playing excellent percentage football and not making any mistakes. We were waiting for the other team to commit them. Because of the quick-strike ability of Griese to Warfield, we had an excellent opportunity to take advantage of these mistakes.

We were facing a Dallas team that was highly seasoned. They had played in the Super Bowl the previous year and lost to the Baltimore Colts in a mistake-filled game. The loss really frustrated them. At the end of the game, Bob Lilly took off his helmet and flung it disgustedly halfway down the field, symbolizing the disappointment of the Cowboys. They had been marked as the team that couldn't win the big one.

The Cowboys were a hot team. They were coming into the Super Bowl off a long winning streak. They turned around in the early part of the season when their coach Tom Landry switched quarterbacks, going from Craig Morton to Roger Staubach. Morton was a highly controversial quarterback who didn't win the Super Bowl the year before. Staubach was a quarterback who had a great amount of ability but scrambled a little too much for Landry's way of thinking. That was the reason why Landry kept going back to Morton. But when he wasn't successful, Landry finally decided to go with Staubach who sparked the Cowboys to the championship.

In our game plan for the Cowboys, we stressed the point that year in and year out they had the best running defense in the game. By the same token, we had established the best running attack. We determined that we would have trouble putting together a consistent running game inside because of the style of defense that the Cowboys played. We agreed that we would have to run outside against them with plays designed to go against the defensive tendencies they had demonstrated in the past. We also figured that we could throw against them. Their pass defense was their biggest problem during the regular season and it was one of the weaknesses that kept them from being a better team than they were. We felt they were vulnerable in the secondary. Our game plan was to attack the middle occasionally, to keep them honest, in an attempt to go wide as much as possible with the run. We designed the game plan to pass on first down. On first-down plays, the Cowboys look for the run and stack their defense to stop it. We were regarded as a running team. The defense they employed in their secondary was designed to stop our outside receivers. They were willing to gamble on leaving our tight end basically free. They felt they would stop our main weapons if they could contain Warfield, Twilley, or Stowe. Our tight ends,

Fleming and Mandich, didn't pose a threat to their way of thinking.

Before the game I could sense that the team was tight. It was obvious on their faces. There was a great amount of pressure on them, a young team playing in the Super Bowl for the first time. I tried very quietly to loosen them up a little, with a remark here and there. Then I told them all not to worry about the Cowboys, but to go out and play our own game. Let's concern ourselves with what we can do on offense and on defense and take the game to them. Let's play as we did all season long.

I thought everything would be all right once the game started. But it wasn't. I noticed that the players were tight. Griese opened the game with a pass, something we wanted to do. It was designed to catch the Cowboys off balance. If the pass was successful, then we figured to get things moving in a hurry. Griese sent Twilley on a down-and-in pattern. But he missed. It was a quick pass play that Griese had connected on hundreds of times. Even though we were stopped on our first series of downs, we still had some opportunities to pick up some momentum early in the contest.

The next time we had possession of the ball, Csonka, following Kiick's block, powered his way on a sweep right for twelve yards to the Dallas forty-six. The play was executed well and it was one reason why I had started Kiick instead of Morris. Kiick had been solid all year and is an excellent blocker. He had played well in the two playoff games against Kansas City and Baltimore. I didn't want to substitute just for the sake of it.

And, besides, I really didn't have that much confidence in Mercury's ability. It was truly more of a lack of knowledge on my part about Morris because he was hurt in the pre-season and was that much behind once the campaign began.

The play gave us excellent field position. Another first down and we would be in field goal range. It would be advantageous to score first in such a pressure-packed game. After Csonka's run, Griese wanted to strike quickly. He called a slant-in pass to Warfield to exploit the first-down Dallas defense that stacked against the run. At the line of scrimmage, Griese surveyed the Cowboys's defense. He alertly noticed that the safety, Cliff Harris, was playing Warfield on the inside while the cornerback, Mel Renfro, was defensing him to the outside. Wisely, Griese checked off. He ordered a running play with Csonka going inside. Griese took the snap. He turned to hand the ball to Csonka. My eyes twinged in disgust. Csonka fumbled! It was the first time he fumbled all season, through sixteen games. It appeared as if Csonka didn't get off the ball real good. The exchange was poor. What hurt was the fact that the mishap occurred on a simple hand-off, one that Griese and Csonka had executed all year long with their eyes practically closed. Csonka really never had full control of the ball. The timing on the exchange was just a split second off. Our tightness was evident.

A fumble at a time like this can really hurt. We never seemed to get untracked. We sort of lost some poise. Our receivers, who are sure-handed, dropped

passes they normally would catch. Griese didn't especially have a good half and he wasn't really effective
the rest of the game. We weren't able to establish the
running game, which would have aided Griese. He
likes to operate off the run in controlling the ball and
the clock. His passing game becomes much more effective this way. Because of the lack of a running game,
we failed along the entire offensive phase of our attack
in not being able to get anything going on first down.
We found ourselves continually in situations where we
had to throw the ball more than we liked. Placed in
this position, Dallas would double their coverage on
Warfield, taking away both the inside and outside
lanes. This presented a problem. So, we tried to take
advantage by passing to our backs. But the Cowboys
exerted good coverage.

Even though we were behind 10–3 at the half, I still
felt that we could come back and win. Our defense had
controlled Staubach. We applied a good amount of
pressure on him. He experienced trouble in trying to
read the coverage and variations that we were using.
Our whole idea was to hold the Cowboys after the second half kickoff and then get our offense going. Surely
we would be able to score a touchdown and pick up
momentum. Then we could put it all together and
emerge with the victory. Being behind seven points
wasn't all that hopeless.

We kicked off and I waited for our defense to take
command. Force Dallas to punt, then we would get the
ball and hopefully go all the way for the tying touchdown. The defense failed. The Cowboys took the kick-

off and moved steadily downfield. They kept the ball for almost six minutes and scored a big touchdown, one that increased their advantage to 17–3. The touchdown put the game out of reach. We never could get back into the game after that. I still had to hope. Yet, the momentum had swung in Dallas's favor.

Defensively, we failed to stop their running attack. When it was all over, they set a new record for yardage gained rushing in Super Bowl play. They did an excellent job of disguising their running plays. Their backs would start out in one direction and wait until our defense committed themselves. Then, quickly, with precision timing, they would cut back against the flow. It left our defenders flatfooted. They had planned their running attack well. They noticed in studying game films that our middle linebacker Nick Buoniconti displayed a tendency to overpursue. He would aggressively commit himself to the flow of the run as it was developing. Duane Thomas, Calvin Hill, and Walt Garrison would start out running with the ball one way, then cut back in the opposite direction. They would pick up their blockers who were waiting for our defensive men as they reacted back. The strategy left gaping holes in our defense. It was actually the worst performance of our club in the two years we had been together. We just never did stop the run, and it made it easy for Dallas the entire game.

Things were going so bad that I was a bundle of frustration on the sideline. It seemed like every time the officials drew the penalty flag out of their pockets and threw it, it was always against the Dolphins. Even though I'm a mild-mannered person on the sideline during a game, I was getting a bit upset. I never say anything to the officials unless I get worked up this way. It got so bad that I tell this story: Somewhere during the fourth peroid I reached the point of being angry. Every time the official threw the flag, I made my anger known. One time after we were penalized, I yelled quite loudly. The official turned, pointed his finger at me, and said:

"Shula, if you open your mouth one more time it is going to cost you!"

Things were going so badly that the last thing I would want to happen was for me to say something on the sideline that would cause the official to penalize me. As he turned to walk away, I noticed that one of our players was slightly out of position. Being frustrated because of our lack of performance, I yelled at him.

"Hey, you dummy, move over."

Hearing that the official whipped around. He thought I was yelling at him. He came storming over toward me, took the flag out of his pocket, and threw it at my feet in front of 80,000 people. I then calmly explained to him that I wasn't shouting at him, but yelling at one of my defensive backs. He accepted my explanation. However, now he, too, was embarrassed. He had already thrown his flag to indicate a penalty.

"Well, it's down. I've got to call it on you."

"Call it on me . . . for what?"

"Coaching from the sidelines."

"What? Coaching from the sidelines. I never heard of that penalty."

"That's what it is . . . coaching from the sidelines."

"What's the penalty?"

"Let's see, coaching from the sidelines is a five-yard penalty."

"This proves that you're stupid. It's a fifteen-yard penalty."

"Shula, for your coaching . . . five yards!"

That's how bad it was. The disappointing thing for me was our performance. Super Bowl VI was a complete failure. The 1971 season, the tremendous accomplishments, the 10–3–1 record, winning the classic playoff game against Kansas City, the AFC championship against Baltimore—all those good things were obliterated by our inept performance against Dallas in what was the most important game this team had ever played.

The toughest thing is talking to the players after a game like this. I told them there was no way we could ever get back what happened to us today. We were the losers in the world championship game. We played poorly and should be embarrassed by our performance. The only way anything good could conceivably come out of this game depended on whether or not we could someday reach back for the experience of having played in the Super Bowl and use this to help us in future Super Bowls. We would no longer be judged by whether or not we won or had winning records during the season. The only way we would be judged again is whether or not we were successful in future Super Bowls. This was asking a lot of them, knowing we could go through the season, have a winning record, get into the playoffs, and win; but unless we got into the Super Bowl and won, that season would be considered a failure. Still, I told them I was proud of them and the tremendous accomplishments they achieved in just two years.

I couldn't help but remember Csonka. He felt dejected. He sat quietly in front of his locker, not really wanting to talk to anyone. He felt terrible about his fumble. He was shook. He thought his fumble cost us the game. I assured him it didn't; the entire team hadn't played up to their capabilities. The Cowboys by being a better football team in this particular game won the world championship and deservedly so. They completely dominated. They were well prepared and executed well. Our losing wasn't a case of being unprepared. We knew what they could do. In fact, they didn't show us anything new and even cut down on their motion. They played a near-perfect game. Fact is, they made only one mistake and that was a fumble by Hill near the end of the game. Up until then they didn't make any mistakes offensively and we made more than we normally make. We went into the game determined to stop the Dallas run and that was what we were unable to do. The only thing we can do is give Dallas credit for what they accomplished against us. All you really have to do is look at what happened. They tore us apart defensively and completely controlled our offense.

The most disappointing thing for me was that we never challenged. Perhaps it was my fault. As the coach, I am responsible for bringing the squad to an emotional peak to play for the world's championship. Maybe I didn't do my job properly. The mistake I made was getting the team ready too early. I should have moved them to an emotional and physical peak right up to the game. Instead, we left a lot of it back on the practice field in Miami. It's a difficult thing for a coach to admit. But I have found that it is much wiser to admit a mistake to yourself and to learn from it. I didn't feel that I had prepared my squad the way it should have been prepared and it was very evident by the way we played. I couldn't place the entire blame on the players. I was the one who was responsible for not charging them to an emotional peak and having them loose for the game.

I could look upon the loss as another step in our development. We had achieved the right to compete for the world championship. We really weren't thinking about winning it. That was a first-time mistake. The Colts in the 1969 Super Bowl felt that they couldn't lose. On the other hand, the Cowboys had played in the Super Bowl the year before and were deeply frustrated because of their poor performance. They had one thing on their minds in preparing to play us. They weren't happy just being in the Super Bowl. Their whole drive and direction was dedicated to winning it.

We lost our edge. Once this happens, it's difficult to get it back. The way we lost pained me. But it also made us face the reality that we were back in the pack, so to speak, with the other twenty-four teams. It was no longer a question of competing for the world's championship but winning it. Still, I couldn't hide my disappointment.

What I dreaded most at that hour was being interviewed on national television. I hated it. I didn't want to. I began thinking of when I had to face those same cameras and millions of people after losing to the New York Jets in the 1969 Super Bowl. Now, three years later, it would be the same thing all over again. How could I explain our performance? We played poorly then and even worse this time. I felt totally embarrassed. People looking at television would be saying, "Hey, here's a two-time loser talking about how his football team lost. He must be getting pretty good at it by now."

I knew I had to be strong to go through with it again. I hoped I had the courage to get me through the interview. It was the low spot of my coaching career. I was in two Super Bowls and was the losing coach both times. It couldn't be any worse. There wasn't any way I could console myself. Only a win would have done that. Tom Landry knows the feeling. He faced the frustrations in the past. Now, as the winning coach, he has accomplished the ultimate. He won the Super Bowl, something I hadn't done. My frustrations would still gnaw at my insides. Only a victory could soothe the pain.

I was dejected, more so than I had ever been in my life. I thought about the statements George Wilson had made and the attacks by Rosenbloom that "Shula can't win the big one." There was only one way to overcome it, I had to win a Super Bowl. I found some comfort in thinking about Vince Lombardi. He had a great winning percentage as a coach, but he was also able to get his teams ready to play in the big games. And they always managed to win. It was the Green Bay Packers who won the game and Vince Lombardi who was the winning coach. I looked up to him because he had accomplished two things—winning often and winning the big ones.

Before I could ever be talked about in the same breath with Vince Lombardi, I would have to show the football world that Don Shula not only could get his team ready to win during the regular season, but also to win the world's championship. I wanted to be the best coach in professional football. I realized that I couldn't be the best unless I was able to get over the hurdle of winning the Super Bowl. I had to win the big one.

12

I bit my lip to control my temper. Finally, I couldn't hold back any more, I began to see red. Feeling flushed, I walked briskly to the other side of the dressing room. The room was hot and crowded with reporters who were busy conducting interviews after the 1972 Super Bowl. For a moment I had forgotten that Dallas had clearly beaten us 24–3. I had a more important matter on my mind, one that caused me to reach a boiling point. My immediate concern was to reprimand one of my players. It couldn't wait until later. I was too angry to wait until everybody had left the room.

One of my aides had whispered in my ear that Mercury Morris was sounding off to the press. He was making derogatory statements that were detrimental to me and the team. There was no way I would let something like that happen. I interrupted my own conversation with a couple of reporters and headed straight for Morris's locker. It was a situation that only I could handle and I knew what I had to do.

I reached Morris's cubicle, which was ringed by reporters. My eyes met his and I pulled him to one side of his impromptu press conference. I looked him straight in the eyes and firmly spoke what was on my mind. I told him point blank that if he had anything to say about me he should tell it to me first. If we can get the matter aired, fine. If not, then he can say it to whomever he wants. He looked at me and didn't answer. Then I asked him to come to my hotel room the next morning.

I realized that Morris wasn't happy about not playing in the game. I certainly wouldn't respect him if he was happy sitting on the bench. But I didn't appreciate one bit the way he opened the matter to reporters from all over the country. Any criticism a player has should be kept within the confines of the organization. It shouldn't be something aired in the newspapers. It's difficult enough keeping every member of a forty-man squad happy. But, if anyone has a bitch, then he should come to me first.

He complained that the longest time he was off the bench was during the playing of the national anthem when he was standing out on the field to be introduced. That, however, wasn't true. He saw some special teams duty, although he didn't get to run from scrimmage in the game. It was my decision not to play Mercury. I wanted to go with the two runners who were steady all season long, Kiick and Csonka. I could have played Morris in the fourth quarter, when the game was hopelessly lost, but I didn't feel that would have done us any good. Nothing would have on this particular day.

I couldn't wait until training camp that summer to begin preparing for the 1972 season. I had to start now, while the loss to Dallas was still fresh and bitter in my mind. I was dying inside all during the remaining minutes of the post-game interviews. I couldn't wait for the reporters to leave. There were hundreds of questions thrown at me and I answered them all as painful as it was. But I wanted answers for myself. What happened in the game was one thing. It was all over. There was nothing I could do in that respect. What I could do was to start changing things for next season. Not when training camp opened in July, but the very next day.

The next morning Morris came to my hotel room for a serious meeting. I was already looking ahead to training camp and the 1972 season. We reviewed the entire situation, what his position was and what I expected from him. He had his opinions and I had mine. I had to get him to see it my way, to believe in what I was doing.

"But, coach, I want to play," pleaded Morris.

"Well, you certainly went about it the wrong way, yesterday," I emphasized.

"I realize that now, and I apologize. Believe me, I didn't intend any harm," explained Morris.

"Very well, but just listen to what I have to say."

"I will, but I just want the opportunity to play, to run with the football the way I know how."

"Fine. If I bring you back next season—and right now there isn't any reason why I don't think you'll be back—the thing that I want to do is find out whether or not you are capable of being a play in and play out full-time player."

"I don't understand," remarked Morris.

"Let me give it to you in a nutshell. You've been primarily a spot player for me in the two years that I've been here. The reason that you've been in that situation is because you've missed so much time. You were hurt so much that I don't know how much I can depend on you."

"But I was ready to play for most of the season," interjected Morris.

"That wasn't the answer. I have to determine how good you really are and how durable, too. I couldn't honestly evaluate those two areas in your role of a spot player. I want to use you more but you have to show me that I can depend on you, game in and game out."

"Coach, just give me the opportunity because I know I can do it," added Morris.

"I promise you you'll get that chance when training camp opens, so be ready for it."

Morris left relieved and determined. I had definite plans for him. I was already designing a three-back system in which I could blend the talents of all three of my running backs, Kiick, Csonka, and Morris. But I had to find out about Mercury first. I was aware of his talent. But I didn't know if he was durable enough to take the pounding; whether or not he could block when Csonka was running the ball to the weak side—

THE WINNING EDGE | 207

something that Kiick does very well. I knew what his strengths were—quick acceleration and speed. It's a powerful weapon in a running back. I wanted to work Morris into our offense because he would add a dimension to our attack that we didn't have. With Kiick and Csonka, we had two big backs, but we didn't have the great outside speed. But with Csonka and Morris, then we had the combination of a big back with power and a back with great outside speed. There was still another combination I could employ, Kiick and Morris. Together, they represent the two best pass receivers I could have in the backfield at the same time, the two best in a possession situation when the opposition knew that we had to throw the ball. In theory it looked good. But I couldn't be sure if it would work until training camp when Morris would be put to the test in the areas that we were concerned about.

I was also concerned about a backup quarterback behind Griese. I wasn't too secure with George Mira who was the No. 2 quarterback. I felt we needed someone with much more experience. Griese was young but I wanted protection behind him in the presence of an older quarterback. I found that help unexpectedly when I was checking the waiver list the following month. To my surprise, Baltimore had placed Earl Morrall's name on the waiver list. It meant that any club could claim him for a hundred dollars. It's a systematic procedure. The last team in order of finish would get first choice and so on up the list until it reached the top team, which at the time was Dallas. Since we finished right behind the Cowboys, we would get the next-to-last chance of claiming him. Surprisingly enough, all twenty-four teams ahead of us passed Morrall up. I knew the reasons. One was his age, which was thirty-seven, and the other was his high salary. I wanted Morrall and I spoke to Joe Robbie about putting in a claim for him.

"Do you think he can help us?" asked Robbie.

"I'm sure he can."

"Well, you had him at Baltimore."

"I know Morrall. He always kept himself in good shape. He has a strong arm and he has an intelligent mind and would fit into our style of play because he understands the importance of the running game."

"Well, then, go get him," exclaimed Robbie.

"There's only one drawback."

"What's that?" snapped Robbie.

"He's carrying a big salary."

"How big?" pressed Robbie.

"He's on the last year of a three-year contract, which we would have to assume. After the 1968 season, when he had such a great year, the Colts rewarded him with a long-term contract."

"Well, maybe we would be better off letting him clear waivers and making a deal with him as a free agent," suggested Robbie.

"That's true, but I don't want to take a chance on losing him."

"How's that possible?" inquired Robbie.

"He has a good business in Detroit and still maintains a home there. He might be influenced to play for a club near home, like Chicago or even Detroit. I'd much prefer to claim him and cut his salary the maximum ten percent we're allowed rather than get caught in a bidding fight for him with other clubs."

"You really feel he's worth the price?" asked Robbie.

"Definitely."

"Well, I'm not worried about his high salary if he'll help bring us a championship," added Robbie.

So I entered a claim for Morrall. I think I surprised Baltimore with the move. In fact, I know I did. The first time he was placed on waivers, a couple of clubs put in a claim and Baltimore withdrew his name. When they tried to get him through a second time, the clubs that previously claimed him passed. That's when I moved in. I'm sure there was a lot of screaming taking place in Baltimore. No team wants to get caught in the position of helping another team in its own conference. They don't even make it a practice to trade with each other. Imagine strengthening your club without giving up anything.

Claiming a veteran like Morrall is one thing. Getting him to sign and play for you is another. I had no assurances that Morrall would want to play any more at his age. However, all the Dolphins were risking was a lousy hundred dollars. I was gambling on my past relationship with Morrall, which was a good one. I'll never forget the job he did for me when we were together in Baltimore in 1968. I felt certain that he would sign with the Dolphins. I knew that he had something left. Baltimore didn't let him go because he couldn't cut it anymore. They had two veteran quarterbacks in Unitas and Morrall. There was a lot of age between them. In fact, Unitas is a year older than Morrall. But, Unitas was something of a legend in Baltimore and you don't put legends on the waiver list. Morrall became expendable.

I spoke to Morrall on the phone and told him before he made up his mind on what he was going to do, to come down and we'd discuss the situation together. He agreed. I told Earl what I expected his role to be. I admitted that I was highly satisfied with Griese and that he was my No. 1 quarterback. What I impressed upon Morrall was the fact that I needed him as solid insurance in case Griese should get hurt. It didn't take much to convince him that the Dolphins were a championship team with an excellent chance to appear in the Super Bowl a second straight year.

In the following few weeks I made another move to strengthen the club. I was looking for more help at wide receiver and secured Marlin Briscoe who had played out his option at Buffalo. The price was high, our No. 1 draft choice in the 1973 college draft. Yet I felt that anytime you can get a receiver of Briscoe's caliber, he certainly is worth a No. 1 draft choice. After all, Briscoe led the American Football Conference in pass receptions the previous season with a weak Buffalo team. I had solid receivers in Warfield and Twilley, but I needed more depth. Otto Stowe had a lot of potential but I was uncertain of his future because of a series of injuries that handicapped him his rookie year.

On paper, the Dolphins already looked stronger than last year's squad. Adding Morrall and Briscoe to the roster accounted for that. They were two proved players. My idea of utilizing a three-back offense of Csonka, Kiick, and Morris certainly made the running attack appear stronger. I had endlessly studied game films in the months before training camp opened and was anxiously waiting to get a better look at two defensive linemen Bob Matheson and Vern Den Herder. I felt they could contribute more to the defensive team's success, but I had to find a spot for them.

I couldn't wait for training camp to open. I felt like a rookie playing in his first game, fired up and anticipating a challenge. Even before July rolled around I was convinced that the Dolphins were a better team than the one that lost to the Cowboys in the Super Bowl a few months earlier. I counted the days until the squad would assemble in the summer heat. All that was needed was the sweat and hard work that would make us a better football team . . . a championship team. I wouldn't settle for less.

It was all there. The squad had gained another valuable year of experience. Coach-player relationships were entering their third year. There would be less mistakes made mentally because of the unfamiliarity with the things we were trying to teach. I also felt that the experience gained by our young players would be very beneficial. Players who were rookies in 1970 were now three-year veterans. My optimism was well founded, especially in the area of defense. The youngsters of 1970 were experienced now. They were still young, but smarter. In 1970, Doug Swift and Mike Kolen were rookie linebackers; Tim Foley, Jake Scott, and Curtis Johnson were rookie defensive backs; Dick

Anderson was only a third-year performer at safety. The only real veteran was middle linebacker Nick Buoniconti. He had played a lot of football over the years but our system was entirely new to him. He had to do a great deal of adjusting from his style of play to discipline himself into the pattern of defense that we demanded.

The sun gets really hot in July in Miami. It beats down and burns and the sweat fills the still air. Yet the only relief in store for the players were the salt pills and finally, blessedly a night's sleep in an air-conditioned room. This was the year. I wanted total emotional involvement from the players. Training camp is where it all begins, where it all happens. Nothing could interfere with what I wanted them to do . . . to win. I wouldn't permit any outside activities to take their minds away from their responsibilities. I wanted them to think football without any distractions. I made it perfectly clear that every player had to concentrate more than ever.

There were three goals that I outlined for the squad. The first was to get into the playoffs. The second was to win the AFC championship and return to the Super Bowl. Then, finally, to win the world's championship, which eluded us the past year. It was all up to them. If they worked hard enough and wanted to win badly enough, they could do it. There was no question in my mind. I knew this was the year.

I didn't have any doubts about Griese getting the job done on offense. He is a remarkable individual. He grasped the system quicker than I ever imagined. It has been only two years since he was introduced to it, which tells you something about his intelligence. He has more talent than any quarterback I have ever coached. And, what's more, he hasn't even reached his prime years yet. Unitas was a great one, but Griese will be even greater.

The only thing I was concerned with on offense was the running attack. I had to make the three-back system work. But, before I could make it go, I had to get the three players involved—Csonka, Kiick, and Morris —to believe in what I was trying to do. They had to understand my theory completely and contribute to make it work. I needed all three to pull together to accomplish it, because each of them had a vital contribution to make. I needed not only their participation, but also their understanding.

I knew it wouldn't be easy. Csonka and Kiick were the establish running backs. It had been this way for the past couple of seasons. Not only that, but also their relationship had carried past the football field. Off of it they were two very close friends. They were an inseparable pair, so known as Butch Cassidy and the Sundance Kid. They had a star image in Miami and their fame was spreading across the league. There wasn't any reason to fault their contribution to the squad, but I knew I needed something else to open up the running attack. That something was Morris.

Mercury reported to camp with anticipation burning in his eyes. He was prepared both mentally and physically. I have never seen him in better physical condition. During our meeting the morning after the Super

Bowl game, I had promised him an opportunity to play. I know he was looking for the chance. And, I gave it to him. If he produced in the manner I hoped he would, then the team would benefit.

In the early phase of camp, it was obvious that Morris would be a factor. His desire was rampant. He showed he was a tough inside runner as well as being a great one outside. His blocking was impressive. He showed that he was capable of picking up the blitzing linebacker on a one-and-one situation. Mercury also revealed that he could block the bigger defensive ends, some standing 6′5″, and bring them to their knees with a vicious body block. In so doing, he cleared the way for Csonka to run to the weak side, very similar to the effectiveness of Kiick. In my mind, and the rest of the coaches, Morris was making it. As he was, the offense itself performed with much more efficiency.

Kiick became very uneasy. He wanted to know what was going on. Morris earned several starts in the preseason games and had looked good. I explained to Kiick that I knew what he could do. I wanted to see whether or not Morris had it for heavy duty. I had given Morris most of the starting assignments. He had responded well and was the talk of the camp. I was certain that my experiment with the three-back system would be fruitful. But the press began to get curious and pressed me on the matter. They wanted to know who was the starter and who was the substitute. I told them there was no such thing, that I had three running backs. I now had several combinations because of the three and could utilize them all in contributing to the success of the team. Some of the writers couldn't see it my way. They thought I was hedging on saying that Kiick had lost his starting job to Morris. I didn't care what they thought because the three-back offense was working.

The acquisition of Briscoe paid dividends early. Stowe, although a highly promising receiver, couldn't be counted upon because of his inexperience. Karl Noonan, a veteran wide receiver, suffered an injury in training camp that sidelined him for the remainder of the year. Twilley, the other veteran pass catcher, was hobbled by an injury and it kept him from practicing the entire pre-season. He wouldn't be ready when the regular campaign began. So, Briscoe got an opportunity to move into the starting line-up although he wasn't familiar with our system. But he worked hard and applied himself and by the time the season opener rolled around, Briscoe was ready. And, for that matter, the entire offense was set, with a few new wrinkles, Briscoe, and the three-back assault.

The other vital area I had to solidify was the defense. Here, too, Den Herder paid dividends. I knew he had potential but I felt he was a couple of years away, simply because of his background. He had played basketball and football for a small college and was lacking in experience. As a rookie last season, he played on the special teams and graded out well. I felt because of his size, he could contribute more to the squad on defense. But, there were two veterans ahead of him, Bob Heinz and Jim Riley. Working him on the defensive line would be a problem. However, if the opportunity came, I was prepared to use Den Herder.

Without any warning, Den Herder got the chance. Almost overnight, too. One afternoon Heinz suffered a fractured vertebra in his upper back. That meant he would be out for at least two months. The next day we were told that Riley, who had a leg problem, would need an operation. The operation on his knee was of the severest nature and he was sidelined for the entire season. I looked in the direction of Den Herder, who was only a second-year man. Asking him to be the No. 1 end was the biggest challenge of his young career. No one worked harder than Den Herder and before training camp ended, I knew I had a starting defensive end.

Because of this situation, we came up with a new defensive twist. It was an innovation that was actually born out of necessity because of the injuries to our linemen. With Den Herder's development, we decided to make full use of veteran Bob Matheson's talents. At first, we used Matheson as a defensive end. That was his primary position when he played with the Cleveland Browns years earlier. He was utilized primarily as a pass rusher. However, we detected that he was capable of being a down lineman. Although he was an effective rusher, he was also strong against the run. We felt that he could create some problems as far as defensive recognition is concerned to the opposing quarterback. So, instead of having Matheson rush the passer, we would have him go from a three-point stance to a two-point stance at the last minute to enable him to drop off and become a linebacker.

We decided to name the innovation the "5-3" because Matheson wore number fifty-three. At times, this would leave us with a three-man rush. But we also could decide to rush another linebacker and drop Matheson off. Now we would have four men rushing the passer and the chance of the element of surprise, creating indecision on the part of the offensive line and the opportunity to get to the quarterback. In the "5-3," Matheson lines up on the outside, usually on the strong side, sometimes in a two-point stance, other times in a three-point stance, depending on what defensive call is given by defensive coach Bill Arnsparger who calls all of our defensives. Middle linebacker Nick Buoniconti makes certain that everybody gets the communication in the secondary and on the line. It is this communication, this team work that gets us started. The "5-3" presented so much more flexibility because of Matheson. He is an exceptional athlete who is capable of rushing the passer or dropping off as a linebacker and knows what it is to get back into coverage and take care of his area of responsibility. By the time training camp ended, we had refined this maneuver and were anxious to test it.

The one remaining area of doubt I was faced with was at the quarterback position. Griese was set, but I needed a strong backup. Morrall did not look good. In fact, he was overshadowed by Jim Del Gaizo, who had been the taxi squad quarterback the year before. Most of the press corps had opted for Del Gaizo. He was a bright young man who could throw the ball very well. Yet, I knew what Morrall could do, despite his poor showing. I also realized that he was playing in pain because of pulled stomach muscles. Still, I could only carry two quarterbacks. One had to go. I decided to keep Morrall. As it later turned out, it was one of the smartest moves I ever made.

There were a lot of questions drumming in my mind when we finished pre-season preparations for the opening of the regular 1972 campaign. What about the three-back offense? Could it really be effective? How about Den Herder? Could he make the big jump from special teams to defensive end? And, the "5-3"—would such an unconventional defense backfire? Would Briscoe help? And what about Morrall? Could he contribute if he were called upon? The questions are always there. But I felt confident about the Dolphins's chances for 1972. I felt I had a championship team. How good remained to be seen. That I'd find out about early.

Our first test was a big one, the Kansas City Chiefs. I had pointed to the game all during training camp. I kept it on the minds of the players: how Kansas City was waiting to get back at us because we defeated them in double overtime for the AFC championship the previous season; the fact that the Chiefs were dedicating their new 80,000-seat stadium; and that the opener was a crucial game for us.

Morris had such a great pre-season that I decided to start him against Kansas City. It was a nationally televised game and Mercury was introduced with the offense. I didn't think much about it at the time. It was a very hot day with the temperature on the playing field over 100 degrees. I alternated Morris and Kiick throughout the game and also created confusion on Kansas City's part with the "5-3" defense. As a result, we managed to defeat the Chiefs easily, 20–10, with their touchdown coming in the final seconds of play. It was a good way to open the season and I was relieved.

However, Kiick wasn't so content. He thought he should have started the game. He felt he deserved it because of his contributions to the club over the years. Because he didn't start and didn't get introduced on television, he felt embarrassed. He was quite upset. Kiick is basically a shy person and one of the last to complain about anything. Not getting the opening game starting assignment bothered him. Now I was faced with a situation where Kiick was unhappy and Morris, who had been unhappy the past two years, was satisfied. And, to further emphasize the situation, one of the local Miami newspapers published a photograph of Kiick sitting on a stool in a corner brooding. I asked at the time if they had that stool saved for the next player who would be unhappy; whether if Morris didn't play the following week they would have his picture on the stool sitting in the corner brooding?

There isn't any way a coach can win in this situation. Everybody wants to play and they all want to contribute. But it was my job to get the most out of players, to utilize their abilities to the maximum. I wanted to start with either Kiick or Morris and then come on with the other one. As the game progressed, I would make the decision as to who would play. If one had the hot hand, I would go with him. If neither did, then I would decide who was best for that position on the field and for the type of plays that we wanted to run. If they both were having hot hands, then so much the better. I knew we were a better team with this system in effect. Naturally, Morris and Kiick aren't in love with it because they realize one has to be on the bench at times. I didn't want anything or anybody to upset the system before it had a chance to prove itself.

It wouldn't have worked without Csonka. He was the constant man who really held it all together, the team man. He could have very easily destroyed our whole picture and our whole unity offensively by taking sides. He had every right to take such a position because of his close relationship with Kiick. It could all have exploded in my face. And then what would have happened to my offense? That's why I had to straighten out the sensitive situation right away. Csonka was the key. It would have been very easy for Csonka to turn up his nose at Morris. He could have shown his resentment in many ways, the least of which was by not blocking for him. But, Csonka grasped the situation and seeing this, Kiick went along with his buddy. Csonka and Kiick accepted Mercury. Their relationship turned out to be a good one. As a matter of fact, I don't know how it could have been any better. When Morris and Csonka lined up together, they would talk to each other, in the same manner in which Kiick would if he was playing. They would give each other hints that would help prepare them for the play. As the season progressed, their relationship grew. When Kiick did something good, the first guy to greet him when he came off the field was Morris. And when

Morris scored a touchdown, the first guy to congratulate him was Kiick. Often on the bench during a game, when the defense was on the field, they would sit together. Over the season the relationship grew and it became a pleasant situation. I know that Kiick wanted to play more and so did Morris. But I also knew what was best for the Dolphins. They finally realized it, too. I wanted to win a championship. And, if it took three backs to do it, then that's the way it was going to be. My offense had three running backs and that's all there was to it. No further explanations were necessary.

The early part of our schedule was arduous. I felt that if we got past it by winning say three out of the first four games, then we would be in excellent position to make a run for the title. Kansas City represented the first hurdle. Beating them was a great start. I didn't anticipate having any trouble the following week against the Houston Oilers. We beat the Oilers easily, 34–13, despite a soggy turf in the Orange Bowl.

However, the game I was most worried about was the next week against the Minnesota Vikings. I looked upon it as the toughest game of the season. The Vikings were a fine team, very physical, and many experts picked them to go all the way. Their quarterback Fran Tarkenton put them on top early with a fine play-action pass on third down and short yardage. He caught our defense off guard and threw a fifty-six-yard touchdown pass to John Gilliam in the opening minutes of play. We spent the next fifty-eight minutes trying to catch up against a very determined Viking team.

We had trouble moving the ball against the rugged Minnesota defense. All we managed in the way of points were a couple of field goals by Garo Yepremian. But we hung tough. With just over four minutes to go in the game, we were down 14–6. We had to get ten points to win—a field goal and a touchdown. The odds were long against a defensive-minded team like the Vikings. But I knew we still had time if we could get something going.

With time running out, I made one of my most important decisions of the year. I gambled on fourth down when we were backed up in our own territory. I disdained ordering a punt, which normally you would do in such a situation, and called for a running play instead. The gamble was made because I felt that in order for us to win the game we had to start doing something positive. If we punted, then there was no telling how long it would have taken us to get the ball back. If the fourth-down gamble backfired, then we'd really be in bad shape deep in our own territory.

Still, I felt it was worth the chance. If we made it, then we had an opportunity to win. Our chances for winning the game, as remote as they may have appeared at the time, all hung on that fourth-down play. Morris got the call and he made the necessary yardage. He started outside and then cut back inside. I was straining to see if he gained enough yards. When it was obvious that he did, I was greatly relieved. Now, I said to myself, if we can only go on from here. I looked up at the clock and knew we had enough time left to win.

We made a first down and then another. But then we stalled. It was another fourth-down situation, only this time it was long yardage. I had two alternatives. Go for it with the percentage against making it, or attempt a fifty-one-yard field goal, which also was a long shot. I liked the chances of making the field goal better. If Yepremian made it, that would give us three of the ten points we needed to win. Yepremian was accurate, and although we were still behind 14–9, I saw everything turning for us. If we could only hold Minnesota after the kickoff, then we'd get that final shot for a touchdown. I was hoping for that final shot.

It was all up to the defense now. They knew what they had to do. They had to bottle up the Vikings, stop them cold without giving up a first down. They accomplished their mission. And they did it by giving us good field position. When the offense took the field, the ball was on our own forty-yard line, giving us room to operate. The clock was a factor. There was 2:29 left in the game. There was time. I told Griese not to hurry, but to keep his head and call the plays the way he was capable under such conditions.

Despite the surrounding pressure, Griese demonstrated such poise that he was oblivious to it all. I think the entire club benefited by this. They all seemed to display the poise that is so necessary for a team to win consistently. Griese needed only sixty-one seconds to get the winning touchdown, a three-yard toss to tight end Jim Mandich. He adroitly moved the squad sixty yards in just six plays. Griese made excellent use of Twilley. I had inserted him into the line-up on the final drive to aid the offense. My thinking was that Griese could use Twilley's experience along with his blocking ability in the event he threw the quick screen pass to Morris. Twilley is an excellent crack back blocker. But instead of the screen, Griese hit Twilley with two big completions, one a down-and-out and the other up the middle on the three-yard line. Griese made an excellent call on the touchdown. Minnesota's defense was primed to stop the run. They placed six defenders up front. Seeing this, Griese called a play-action pass and calmly tossed the ball to Mandich in the end zone. It was a smart call.

I now had the three victories I felt were necessary in the early part of the schedule. The Viking victory was most satisfying. It demonstrated how we didn't collapse even though we fell behind and had trouble scoring against them. We never panicked and stayed with what we had, making the big plays when we had to. This game demonstrated how much character the team had and how far we came along in the short span of three years. Maintaining poise and coming from behind are characteristics of a championship team. I knew we could go all the way after this game. The way the squad reacted in the face of adversity told me a lot of things.

Buoyed by the Minnesota victory, we then had to face the New York Jets in New York. A triumph now would further propel our championship aspirations. The Jets were our biggest rivals for the Eastern Division title. We were 3–0 while they were 2–1. If we lost, we would be tied for first place. If we won, then we would jump two games ahead of them. In essence, the contest itself was worth two games in the standings. As usual, Joe Namath, the Jets's great quarterback, represented our major concern. If you can stop Namath, you pretty much can stop the Jets and control the game. Namath was a big challenge since only two weeks before he had put on a tremendous passing performance in shattering Baltimore's zone.

Our plan was to confuse Namath who is as good as any quarterback around in reading defenses. We didn't give him any one thing but a number of variations. And we succeeded in complicating him. The "5-3" was especially confusing to him. He didn't know when Matheson was going to rush him or drop back in a linebacker's role. This seemed to bother Namath all afternoon. At other times we'd put in a fifth defensive back and pull out a linebacker in obvious passing situations. The way the secondary kept moving around had to confuse Namath. Our whole thinking was to give Namath something else to worry about. If you have him in a guessing game, then you have an edge. Sometimes it's the winning edge, that something extra you look for.

In using a lot of zone variations, we succeeded in putting a blanket on Namath. Not that you will ever completely shut him out. But we effectively controlled him, limiting him to only 152 yards. Even though the Jets scored first, we took charge right afterward and by the third quarter had the game practically wrapped up. The victory was one of magnitude. Instead of coming out 3–1 or 2–2 in our first four games, we were now 4–0 with a two-game lead. Then I realized that this club was destined for a great year. We overcame the crucial early part of our schedule flawlessly, winning every game and maturing in the process. I didn't have to look back anymore. Everything was ahead of us now.

I felt good. Real good. Winning our first four games was more than I had hoped for. Not that I don't go out on the field expecting to win every time. I am a positive thinker and I always play to win. That's what the game is all about. But a coach has to be realistic. A great amount of analyzing is necessary. You look at a situation and you weigh the facts. You play to win but you know that winning every game is virtually impossible, even though your game plan is designed toward that purpose. You work toward that goal with endless hours of preparation. Yet, very few coaches have ever attained the perfect season.

After the first month of the season I wasn't thinking along those lines. There are too many extenuating circumstances over the long season. Injuries are the most overriding factor. In analyzing our first four games, I was pointing realistically toward three victories. The only easy win I had anticipated was Houston. The other three—Kansas City, Minnesota, and New York—were acknowledged as very tough games with the final outcome questionable. The fact that we prevailed in all four games had me thinking championship very seriously. I knew then that the squad had what it took to go all the way.

Six of the remaining ten games on the schedule were

set for the Orange Bowl. Naturally, it's a nicer feeling playing at home than on the road. At least you know which side the fans are on. The first of the six games was San Diego. The Chargers were in a rebuilding season under coach Harlan Svare. A defensive-minded coach, Svare had assembled a tough front four— Deacon Jones, Ron East, Dave Costa, and Lionel Aldridge. They figured to give us trouble up front. Early in the game, Griese called a bootleg pass and rolled out to his right. He was looking to hit Kiick down the middle.

That was the last time I saw Griese on his feet. East hit Griese low and Jones got him high. Griese crumbled to the ground. My heart began to beat rapidly. I knew he was hurt badly. He lay on the ground writhing in pain. I rushed onto the field staring at Griese. "Get up," I kept repeating to myself. "Dear God please make him get up." I realized he was much more seriously hurt than I first imagined. Why did this have to happen? Why to Griese, who was heading for his best season? Why now when we were on the way to a championship? As they carried Griese off the field on a stretcher, I couldn't help but feel a little sorry for myself. It wasn't that I was selfish. I just wanted so very much for this team to win it all. I knew this was their year. But, there wasn't any time for remorse. We were in a critical situation. I looked at Morrall. I called him over and said, "It's all up to you now, Earl."

As Morrall headed on the field to pick up the pieces, I couldn't help but think what a spot he was suddenly on. He had a bad pre-season. Del Gaizo had actually outperformed him. Everybody felt that I had kept Morrall on the squad because of personal reasons. But I had a feeling about Morrall. I remembered how valuable he was when he played for me at Baltimore. Call it faith. Call it intuition. But I decided to have Morrall behind Griese instead of Del Gaizo. Along with Morrall, I, too, was suddenly and dramatically put on the spot before 80,000 people along with the critics in the press box. It was my decision, and mine alone, to keep Morrall. And because of this the fortunes of the Dolphins were now placed squarely in his hands. I was hoping for the Morrall of 1968, the Morrall who won fifteen games. I didn't know what to expect. But I felt he had the experience and the ability to get the job done. The challenge he now faced was enormous.

In the huddle, Morrall asserted himself. He simply said, "Let's keep it going." The squad felt his leadership qualities at that moment. They didn't let down but responded to their new leader. I could see it happening. Morrall took charge and was outstanding. He understood the importance of the running game. He alternated the run and the pass effectively and kept the Chargers off balance. He displayed his accuracy by throwing two touchdown passes. The offense functioned smoothly, as if Griese were still operating at quarterback. As the game continued, I could see that my faith in Morrall would be fulfilled. He led us to a 24–10 victory, which kept our winning momentum going. It was extremely important for Morrall to get established in this way. He had almost an entire season to play.

At this point I wasn't concerned about going through the season unbeaten. All I wanted was to maintain the winning edge. With a 5–0 record, we were the team to catch. When I learned that Griese had suffered a broken ankle and would be sidelined for the rest of the campaign, I was content just to keep one step ahead of the next team. As long as we won our division and qualified for the championship play-offs, then we could start thinking about the Super Bowl. Right now there were nine more games to play. A lot could happen in that time. I was determined that it wouldn't be bad.

I saw positive signs in the San Diego game that eliminated such fears. Like the Minnesota game, the results of the San Diego one did much to contribute to our success. Against the Vikings, we demonstrated poise and the ability to come from behind against a tough club. Against the Chargers we displayed another dimension—character. The squad could have very easily folded and given up against San Diego when Griese was carried off the field. Instead, the players pulled together and worked extra hard to get the job done and keep the momentum going. The important thing was that they believed in Morrall.

As the season progressed, the club realized they could win without Griese. It was like a new challenge to them. Everybody questioned whether we could win without him. They felt that we'd lose our edge and would begin to taste defeat. I emphasized to the squad that now, more than ever, they would have to prove they were truly champions. Facing adversity and overcoming it was part of being champions. We had to show the league that we were more than a one-man team even though we lost a key player like Griese. Morrall got them going against San Diego and I knew then he could keep them going. The important thing was to approach each game as it came without looking past it to the following week's opponent. That would be dangerous and could easily provide a pitfall.

It almost occurred against the Buffalo Bills, a team we figured to beat easily. The game was too close as far as I was concerned, 24–23. It provided us with our sixth victory, the closest of the year. This was the first game we started without Griese, and maybe everyone just was a little bit tight. We were penalized a great deal and had some close calls go against us. I lost my temper on one of them, one of the very few times I have done this throughout my coaching career. Morrall had tossed a swing pass to Morris, which was tipped by a Buffalo linebacker. The Bills covered the ball on our thirty-six-yard line and the referee awarded them possession. He claimed that play was a lateral and not a pass. I was furious. I screamed at the referee, trying to get his attention. In my eagerness, I pulled him toward me. Automatically we were penalized fifteen yards for unsportsmanlike conduct. I was wrong in touching the official, but I knew I was right in that he made a bad call.

When we beat Baltimore for our seventh victory, there was a feeling by many that we might possibly go undefeated. After all, the season was halfway over. Still, I didn't give it much thought. But I was constantly asked, week after week as we kept winning, whether the pressure was building. I don't honestly feel that it was. We very seldom ever talked about what we had accomplished. What happened was behind us. Quite naturally we were pleased that we were the only team that hadn't lost a game. It had been that way after the third week of the season. But we didn't spend a lot of time thinking about our success. Instead, I made certain that the squad concentrated on the team we were going to play next and what we had to do to win.

I didn't want the squad thinking about going through the season unbeaten. The more that fact was minimized the better. I fully realized that we were capable of winning. But I didn't want to make it an emotional thing. I felt it would be best to keep it low-keyed. Whenever we didn't play exceptionally well, as against Buffalo, I treated the game like a loss in our team meeting on Tuesday. We discussed the errors we made and how we had to correct them if we expected to keep on winning. We actually talked about such games more negatively than positively. We kept on trying to learn and looking for things even though we were winning. We made corrections where they were needed. We wanted to make the players realize that possibly we might have been fortunate to get by this particular game and we might not have the same opportunity to get by the next week. This is one of the reasons we were able to continue to win week after week. Keeping the players concentrating on each game took the pressure off the winning streak and an unbeaten season.

I had to keep the players' minds riveted on winning.

I had to guard against complacency. It can happen to a team that is going good. I pointed to upsets that were happening around the league. Teams that were supposed to win were rudely upended. I used this to motivate. I didn't want to be the victim of an upset and then have the squad wake up and start playing tougher the next week. We talked about how upsets were good when you read about them happening to other clubs. It made us aware that we were in a tremendous struggle in our drive to be the best team in football. This awareness was necessary. It was helpful in the overall success of the team.

The ninth victory was especially meaningful to me. Not because we routed New England 52–0, but because it was the hundredth victory of my coaching career in regular season play. It might not seem like a lot at first, but it held special significance in that I was the first coach in the history of professional football who had ever won that many games in his first ten years. Anytime you're the first and history is associated with it, you have to feel a sense of achievement. And I was happy with the accomplishment. I tried to remain as subdued as possible over the honor. The magnitude of it couldn't have been accomplished by me alone. It took two very necessary ingredients—excellent assistants and outstanding players. And I might add organizations. I had all three components in Baltimore and now in Miami. Individual honors are great to attain. But I feel that total satisfaction can only be fully enjoyed if it occurs within the framework of a championship. I didn't want to savor it until I had won the

Super Bowl. Finishing the regular season unbeaten was another feeling of satisfaction. It hadn't been accomplished in the NFL since the Chicago Bears won all their eleven games in 1942. But I didn't have time to relish the 14–0 record we had produced. The Super Bowl was the ultimate goal. But first we had to get through the playoffs.

The first-round opponent was the Cleveland Browns. They were the wild-card entry and a team that was lightly regarded by many. However, I have learned that you never take a playoff team lightly, no matter who they are. If they reach the playoffs, they have to be good. I remember only too well in 1964 when I took a heavily favored Baltimore team to Cleveland in a similar situation. We were picked to win by two or three touchdowns and were soundly beaten 27–0. I knew the Browns would be tough. Art Modell, the owner, was psyching his team the week before the game in Miami. He said he was just thankful his team had qualified for the playoffs. He just hoped they would play a good game against the Dolphins because we were a far superior team.

But I wasn't being lulled to sleep. Not this time. I knew the Browns would give us all we could handle. They have always prided themselves in championship play. This time was no exception. They gave us one of our toughest games of the year. In fact, we were trailing 14–13 with just seven minutes left to play. We couldn't do much offensively against their fired-up defense. In reality, our defense had kept us in the game. They played alertly and intercepted five of Cleveland's passes. Then, too, the special teams scored our only touchdown in the first period. Rookie Charlie Babb scooped up a blocked punt on the six-yard line and went in for a touchdown. Yet, Morrall pulled the offense together in that final drive and moved the squad eighty yards in just six plays to give us a hard earned 20–14 victory.

Even though we beat Cleveland, I was concerned the week we were to play Pittsburgh for the AFC championship. Morrall had done a tremendous job filling in for Griese. I couldn't have asked for more. No coach could. He had started ten games and won all of them. He was largely responsible for our offense continuing to move the way it was capable during the long time Griese was on the sidelines. However, as the season drew to an end, it was evident to me that we were having more and more trouble moving the ball with any degree of consistency. It troubled me. I knew we couldn't afford a breakdown in this phase, especially if we hoped to reach the Super Bowl. I realized that the solution to the problem would be a healthy Griese.

I watched Griese closely on the practice field working out each day. He was moving a little better with each day and I thought about giving him some playing time. I was able to do it in the final game of the season against Baltimore. It was good having him back, even if only for a brief period. Yet, I knew he wasn't quite ready for the physical rigors of a full game. So, I picked Morrall to start against Pittsburgh, the final step before the Super Bowl.

I had mixed emotions going into the game against the Steelers. Their coach, Chuck Noll, was one of my former assistants in Baltimore. He is a bright coach and I wasn't surprised at the job he did in bringing Pittsburgh to a championship level in a short time. I have always admired the Steelers's owner, Art Rooney. I have more respect for him than any other owner in professional football because of what he has contributed to the sport. He is also a tremendous human being. You talk about goodness and you begin with Art Rooney. You talk about generosity and once again you start with Art Rooney. Before the game I talked briefly with him. I told him that I was very happy we had the opportunity to play against each other in this important championship game.

The Steelers scored first. And very quickly. It took them only four plays to score a touchdown and we were suddenly behind, 7–0. We had trouble moving on offense. In fact, Morrall couldn't advance past the Steelers's forty-nine-yard line. However, we managed to score on an alert play by punter Larry Seiple. Instead of punting, Seiple fooled everyone by running for a big first down. Hoping to set up a return to the right side, the Steelers rushed only one defender at Seiple. Seeing this, Seiple evaded the rush and took off down field, reaching the Steeler twelve-yard line before he was stopped. Two plays later, Csonka scored from nine yards out on a swing pass from Morrall.

At half time, the score was 7–7. I didn't like the way we looked on offense. It was almost identical to the situation I experienced in the 1969 Super Bowl game against the Jets. Morrall was the quarterback for me then. This time, however, I made up my mind to switch. I decided to go with Griese. I simply made the decision because I thought it was the thing to do. It had nothing to do with the 1969 Super Bowl decision. All my decisions are based on what I think is best for the team at the time I have to make a decision. I walked over to Griese who was sitting in front of his locker.

"Are you ready to go in and take over?" I asked.

"I'm ready," he replied.

"Okay, then you start the second half," I told him.

I felt the switch to Griese might get the offense moving. If he succeeded, fine. If not, I could always go back to Morrall late in the game. But I had to do something to get some points on the board. It was a move I had to make.

I walked over to Morrall. What I had to tell him was hard. It was tough to inform him that I was starting Griese in the second half. He had done the job all season long and I was appreciative beyond words. But I had to do what was best for the team. I had to think only of winning and put sentiments aside.

"Earl, I'm starting Bob in the second half," I said.

"That's your decision," he answered.

"I feel it's the best thing to do," I replied.

"If you need me I'll be ready," he remarked.

His reaction made me feel better inside.

Griese got us going. He went into action with the Steelers ahead 10–7, following a field goal early in the third period. He sparked us to two touchdowns to provide the difference in our 21–17 triumph. We had won the AFC championship for the second consecutive year. Our record now was 16–0. But it wouldn't mean anything if we didn't win our next game. That was the Super Bowl.

13

The spring meeting of the National Football League in Scottsdale, Arizona, this past April didn't appear too exciting. There were a number of matters that I was concerned with—the two-point conversion, sudden death, and expansion. However, nothing significant was changed although there were lengthy discussions on each subject. Ever since I became a head coach with the Baltimore Colts in 1963, I had always looked forward with a great deal of anticipation to attending league meetings. They provide an excellent opportunity to meet with other coaches and owners and express ideas on how to improve the game. These meetings have helped professional football become the game it is today. The exchange of ideas and suggestions on how to improve the product are invaluable and often quite productive when rules or conditions are changed. But aside from the business matters, the meetings also provide an opportunity to socialize with the other coaches, owners, and their wives. It gives everybody a chance to relax away from the pressures of the season.

The Camelback Inn provided an excellent setting for the meetings. It is a posh resort and offered any number of activities for the guests. I like to play golf whenever I can, but I didn't get much of a chance to do so because of the meetings that were scheduled every day. Still, I did manage to get in a round or two. Most of my time was spent attending the meetings and being interviewed by writers who hadn't talked to me since the Super Bowl game just three months before.

Early in the week I was taken by surprise. Don Klosterman approached me at one of the meetings and said that Carroll Rosenbloom wanted to meet with me at my convenience.

"When does he want to get together?"

"Any time you say."

"Well, let's do it as soon as possible."

"What do you suggest?"

"How about right after the morning meeting?"

"That sounds good. I'll tell Carroll."

I immediately thought about the last time I tried to talk to Rosenbloom. That was three years ago in Hawaii. The spring meeting of the league was taking place at the time. It was the first league meeting I had attended since I left Baltimore and took over as head coach of the Dolphins. I saw him at a cocktail party and approached him. I attempted to shake his hand and thank him for everything he had done for me during my seven years in Baltimore and to say that I hoped we could in some way remain friends. He completely ignored me and turned his back on me and refused to say one word. This hurt me. I couldn't do anything but turn around and walk away.

Ironically, the room where we met at the Camelback was named the Peace Pipe Room. I really didn't know what to expect of the meeting. I could only hope that it would be successful. Klosterman got between Carroll and me and put his arms around both of us. Then he spoke.

"Why don't the both of you shake hands and get all these things that have been happening in the past out of the way."

I looked at Rosenbloom and extended my hand. But I didn't say anything. I waited for him to speak. Then he broke the silence that had lasted for three years.

"Don, let bygones be bygones."

"That's okay with me but an awful lot has happened in the last three years."

"Well, I was quite disappointed when you left the Colts while I was out of the country."

"I went through the proper channels. When I had the opportunity to talk with Miami I asked your son Steve for permission and he granted it."

"I felt that you took advantage of Steve."

"Why do you say that?"

"You and I had always talked privately together on important matters."

"That's the way it had been. But our relationship had deteriorated our last year together. I didn't enjoy the same feelings I once had."

"Well, we don't have to look back at the past any-more."

"Hopefully we can look away."

"It would be nice."

"I'm glad that we had the opportunity to finally sit down and talk."

The meeting was over. It hadn't lasted long. It was strange sitting there talking to Rosenbloom again after not having done so for over three years. At least, now, we had established lines of communication. It took a great deal for Carroll Rosenbloom to sit down and talk with me. I realize that. I am happy that we were able to get together after all these years, which were bitter ones for me. I'd hate to think we could go through life feeling the way about each other that we had for three years.

I do appreciate all the things that Rosenbloom did for me, especially in giving me the opportunity to be-come a head coach. I have thanked him for that. I was just so disappointed over the past three years during which I was subjected to one type of personal attack after the other. I hope now that it will finally end. Any-time anything comes up in the future we could hope-fully at least sit down and talk about it. The lines of communication are the only way our differences will ever be resolved. I definitely think our meeting was a step in the right direction. I can only hope that our re-lationship will, over a period of years, return to nor-malcy.

The only way any problem can be solved is through discussion. It's true of life in such avenues as government, industry, football, and even marriage. I'd like to think that in the future anytime Rosenbloom and I see each other we will be able to shake hands and talk about what's good for professional football. I know that Rosenbloom is very much interested in that. I'd also like to renew some type of relationship between our families. I know he thought a great deal of Dorothy and our family before we left Baltimore. And we certainly felt the same way about his wife, Georgia, and their family.

But, you never really know what the future will bring. After the meeting, there were some things written in the newspaper that disturbed Rosenbloom, particularly the matter of who requested the meeting, and because a number of things that happened in the past were again brought up publicly. I know that both Carroll and I hope these things will be forgotten now that we have been able to sit down and communicate. We anticipate that our relationship will be just talked about in terms of the present and that people will not continue to bring up a lot of the things that are very distasteful about the past.

14

Inscribed on the shank of our Super Bowl rings are
four words that have immense meaning to me—Perfect
Season and Winning Edge.

The words Perfect Season, naturally, sum up the
1972 season put together by the Miami Dolphins, a his-
tory-shattering performance that may never be dupli-
cated. The words Winning Edge represent a concept
for achieving victory that I brought with me to Miami.
They are linked together, much as a ring links man
and woman together in marriage.

The words Winning Edge, and the idea that goes
with it, may be my most important contribution to the
Miami Dolphins. I feel you set a goal to be the best
and then you work every waking hour of each day
trying to achieve that goal.

The ultimate goal is victory, and if you refuse to
work as hard as you possibly can toward that aim,
or if you do anything that keeps you from achieving

that goal, then you are just cheating yourself. I feel that way about athletics, but more importantly I feel that way about life in general. And I have always felt that way. When I joined the Dolphins in 1970, I knew I was joining a team that had never had a winning season and had no tradition to fall back on. I wanted to be able to translate what I felt into meaningful terms for them—terms they could easily understand and that, by being catchy, would stick with them. In that way, they might have a substitute for tradition. The phrase I coined was "Winning Edge."

To make the phrase more visible, we had a poster made and placed prominently in our meeting room at Biscayne College, where it hangs in full sight of every player. The top of the poster has the words "How To Get The Winning Edge" in large block letters. Underneath, the poster is sectioned into four squares, one for each letter in the word "Edge" with a definition of what each letter means. "E" represents Extra Study, "D" is for Determination, "G" is for Gassers, and the final "E" is for Extra Effort. We hope the players think about the whole concept of the Winning Edge and the component parts that hopefully will produce the edge that enables us to win.

Extra study, determination, gassers and extra effort cover three areas that I feel are keys to success—mental, physical and emotional.

We want the Dolphins to be better prepared mentally than our opponents by realizing the importance of not making mental errors in a game. A player can be the greatest physical specimen and execute flawlessly in practice but if he can't carry out the detail of his assignment in a stress situation during a game on Sunday afternoon he really isn't of significant value. The main thing we try to find out about a player before we draft him is whether or not he has the ability to learn. We want to know as much as possible about his mental capacity. We also give psychological tests. These are football oriented and disclose determination, aggressiveness and eight or nine other traits. They tell us about the player and how we can handle him when he comes under the influence of coaching. It all fits into the classroom atmosphere of a teacher-to-pupil relationship.

Once the players are on the field, we put them into teaching situations. After the subject is taught, we give them endless hours of review and repetition in an effort to reduce execution to habit rather than having the player think about what he has to do. This enables him to execute to the maximum degree. If we have done our job and the player does his, it could produce the Winning Edge in a game.

I also like to have an edge against any opponent in physical conditioning. On the face of it, physical abilities are just about equal. Linemen have to be a certain size, possess certain speed and have certain strength. Linebackers have certain requirements and so do running backs. All things being equal, the team that has the best conditioned athletes and the fastest ones will have the Winning Edge. I'm a stickler on condition. It's so extremely important in a hot city like Miami, where we play half of our games. We've pushed our squad to have more stamina and more endurance than our opponents. We've been able to sell this idea to our team and we've been able to prove to them how this actually has helped us to win some games.

When I first arrived in Miami I wondered about the advisability of working the squad in the heat of south Florida. I had deliberated about opening a training camp in the cooler mountain region of North Carolina. I actually preferred the cooler climate to the heat of Florida. But I talked with a number of medical men and other coaches who had trained their teams in hot climates and I reached the conclusion that we would be better off training in south Florida. Before long we discovered that the players rounded into shape faster in the torrid heat. The teams that we played in the early pre-season games just weren't in as good physical condition as we were. This was very noticeable in the fourth period of the game.

During that first year I remember stopping practice a couple of times during the morning drills. It was terribly hot and there weren't any breezes stirring to offer relief. I ordered ice to be brought on the field and I allowed the players to quench their thirst by drinking Gatorade or by sucking on an ice cube. But that's the only time I did it. I haven't done it since and our players now know that practices will not be stopped and they work hard with that in mind. They realize the value of condition. We take a lot of pride in working in the heat, realizing fully that it is all worth while, every bead of perspiration. We've played some games in the Orange Bowl when the temperature on the artificial turf was anywhere from 120 to 140 degrees. Physically, we can take it, an edge that we've gained. I know our players can't wait for the teams from the north to come down and play late in the season. They actually want a hot day. They are aware that the opposing linemen, who haven't been doing a lot of running under these conditions, will have to run and chase early in the game against our outside running attack. They know it will tire them and in the fourth quarter we will come on stronger physically.

The third edge I like to gain is in the area of emotions. I demand total involvement from our players. After God and family, the only other thing that's important is what the Dolphins do on game day. That requires total involvement. I'd hate to think that we'd ever lose a game because we weren't involved as much as the other team. Emotional involvement means everything. If there are any statements that I totally disagree with, statements that I don't ever want attributed to me, they are: "Our opponents wanted the game more than we did," or "They were more ready to play the game than we were," or "Their emotions ran higher than ours."

We became fully aware of how important the emotional edge is as our winning streak was building during the 1972 season. Teams that we were playing against were at a fever pitch. Even though they were out of the championship race, they felt it would be a feather in their cap if they could knock off the undefeated Dolphins. We had to be ready to play. We had to realize what the opposition wanted to do and then

THE WINNING EDGE | 249

prepare ourselves so that our emotions reached higher than the emotions of our opponent. We wanted the edge here too.

The overall result, if we have gotten our message across and our players have followed through, is that somehow we will get the Winning Edge—the edge in competition that will win for us, either with the players on our offensive team, the players on our defensive team, or the players on our special teams. How we get that edge or who gets it for us doesn't matter. What does matter is that we get it.

The Winning Edge, then, is the standard for any player trying to become a member of the Miami Dolphins. Not only must he understand the concept, he must be willing to make the sacrifices necessary to make the standard produce the end result for himself; to gain an edge over his opponent.

It is my feeling that the concept of the Winning Edge and our ability to drive it home to our players helped produce the Perfect Season we experienced in 1972. As a matter of fact, I doubt very much whether we could have gone through the season undefeated if every player on our roster had not believed the concept and contributed what he could to the over-all effort.

Now we hope that the Winning Edge can help us climb to another plateau. It wasn't long after the 1972 season ended before people began asking what the Miami Dolphins could do for an encore. It was easy to quip, in light of the 1972 season, that we could always do it again. But that, admittedly, was only a quip. It took a chance meeting with Mrs. Marie Lombardi, wife of the late and great coach of the Green Bay Packers and Washington Redskins, to help shove me toward a more viable target.

In talking with Marie, I couldn't help remember the standard of excellence Vince Lombardi had achieved with the Packers. He had directed the Packers to so many successes that their ability to achieve what they set out to do became a hallmark not only for professional football organizations but organizations throughout all society. In every walk of life, leaders began to look to Vince Lombardi and the Green Bay Packers, exploring the methods by which the man and the team reached the goals they did. In that way, Vince Lombardi and the Green Bay Packers took their message beyond pro football.

The more I thought about Vince Lombardi's achievements the more determined I became that an encore was only a small part of the entire target. What we want to dedicate ourselves to is establishing a standard of excellence in the future, just as the Packers did in the past.

That is the challenge. For the Miami Dolphins. And for Don Shula.